Donated by...

The

Jost-Ore

Contemporary Studies in Literature

Eugene Ehrlich, *Columbia University*
Daniel Murphy, *City University of New York*
Series Editors

Mark Twain

a collection of criticism edited by Dean Morgan Schmitter

McGraw-Hill Book Company

New York • St. Louis • San Francisco • Auckland • Düsseldorf • Johannesburg
Kuala Lumpur • London • Mexico • Montreal • New Delhi • Panama • Paris
São Paulo • Singapore • Sydney • Tokyo • Toronto

Buffalo
September,
1975

For Amy Morgan

123456789MUMU7987654

Library of Congress Cataloging in Publication Data

Schmitter, Dean Morgan, comp.

Mark Twain: a collection of criticism

  (Contemporary studies in literature)
  CONTENTS: Biography and general criticism: Wagenknecht, E. The matrix. Hubbell, J. B. Mark Twain.
Tanner, T. The pond of youth. Jones, H. M. The
pessimism of Mark Twain. Tuckey, J. S. Mark Twain's
later dialogue: The "me and the machine".—[etc.]
—Selected bibliography (p.   )

  1. Clemens, Samuel Langhorne, 1835–1910. I. Title.
PS1331.S25   818'.4'09   74-19111
ISBN 0-07-055394-7

Preface

Hardly any fact or opinion about Mark Twain or any of his writing has escaped scholarly or critical attention, but by far the largest share of concern has been concentrated on his personality and a few of his literary works. The selections printed in the following pages are limited to essential information and studies of his most popular and important writings.

The aim has been to give a general introduction to readers and students interested in Mark Twain and his work. Consequently, material has been chosen on both general and specific topics. For convenience, the material has been divided into two parts. Part I contains selections on Twain's biography, his literary career, and on two general themes in his writing. Part II is made up of criticism of the major titles, as many as space would allow.

Readers interested in investigating Mark Twain's career further will find studies on almost all possible aspects of his life and writings in the bibliographical section that follows the criticism section. The necessity of choosing from so many possibilities influenced the decision to limit the bibliography to books rather than to include contributions to journals, which, for many readers, might not be readily available. However, all the entries in the *Bibliographies* subsection *Writings about Mark Twain* (p. 148) list journal articles.

D.M.S.

Columbia University
November, 1974

Contents

Dean Morgan Schmitter

Introduction: Mark Twain and the Pleasures of Pessimism

Samuel Langhorne Clemens was a very funny man who has become a legendary figure, an American hero, under his pseudonym Mark Twain. Other Americans have been almost as funny and have been forgotten, for humor is a fragile product that neither ages nor travels well. But Mark Twain had a rare combination of gifts that promises to keep him permanently in the American consciousness both as a personality and as a writer. His best work is ageless although not everyone has found the same hilarity in the "Jumping Frog" story or in the high comedy of the disappearing spoons in *Huckleberry Finn*. The most sympathetic readers may find the humor forced at times in *Innocents Abroad* and *Roughing It* without succumbing to the conclusion, as some of his contemporaries did, that he was rambunctious and crude instead of comic.

Humor played a part in making Mark Twain the national figure that he was, but only a part. The tall tales and funny stories that brought him to national attention would not alone have brought him such affection from his contemporary readers nor sustained him for long with new generations. He was also involved in the large and small details of American life, and he extended his likes and dislikes to the European scene, all the way back to the Middle Ages. For the most part, he maintained his popular reputation by packaging serious material in humorous wrappings, or, at least, in the cadences of a man who had learned his business in the humorist's trade. In just this way, his friend and sympathetic critic, William Dean Howells, hoped he would go down to posterity. "What we all should wish to do," he said, when the American hero was at the height of his popularity, "is to keep Mark Twain what he has always been: a comic force unique in the power of

1

charming us out of our cares and troubles, united with as potent an ethic sense of the duties, public and private, which no man denies in himself without being false to other men.''[1] Howells was shrewdly aware of how Mark Twain combined comic style with serious commentary, and he differs from later critics only in the emphasis he gives to the humor.

In the popular view, Mark Twain is still the humorist who also indulged in commentary on human foolishness. And these practices combined with other qualities, some obvious and others mysterious, to endow him with the reputation of the quintessential American, different from a mere public figure or writer, as though he summed up in his person and his work a distillation of our most typical qualities. Part of this mystique will yield to reason, but a larger part will not, for even so mercurial and contradictory a person as Mark Twain cannot represent so impure a compound as the typical American. Yet we recognize enough of the national character in this image of Twain to give us a sense of ourselves, or, more likely, a myth that Americans cherish and that Europeans accept.

No doubt metaphor carries more weight than fact in the observation that Mark Twain was born and reared in the very heart of the nation, on the great river that flows down through its center; for it is certainly true that the special vitality of commerce and the adventure offered by life on the banks of the Mississippi were less typical of mid-country America than was the enclosed life of thousands of inland villages and towns scattered over the central Mississippi basin. Although Mark Twain profited from the stimulation of the comparatively exotic river, he also had, as a prototypical American, the advantages of poor but honest parents, little formal education, and early experience at modest jobs. Later, he shared in the mobility that characterized a restless nation, indulging in several adventurous years as a river pilot, followed by a footloose period in the knockabout frontier regions of the west. By nature, he was tempestuous, profane, opinionated, irreverent, and in permanent possession of a sympathy for the underdog and of an itch for wealth. The notion that Americans are typically cut from such cloth is probably no more inaccurate than are most national stereotypes.

As time has passed and we have been able to see Mark Twain whole, we have come more and more to recognize that his talent to entertain, which had been rehearsed and polished during his early career, found in the 1870s and 1880s its natural partner and settled down to an unstable marriage. The partner was pessimism, that melancholy view of the human situation that, hoping for joy and finding it

[1]From a review written in 1901 and included in *My Mark Twain: Reminiscences and Criticisms,* ed. Marilyn Austin Baldwin, (Baton Rouge: Louisiana State University Press, 1967), p. 162.

unjustified, turns more and more to a criticism of things as they are. In Mark Twain this view was rationalized into a profound mistrust of the virtue of hope, nagged by a constitutional inability to discount it completely. Unfortunate as this combination may have been for Mark Twain's personal tranquility, it gave to his humor purpose and point, fulfilling Coleridge's sober dictum that laughter "is equally the expression of extreme anguish and horror as of joy." Recognizing the deep seriousness in his work, current criticism differs from Howell's hope that Mark Twain's comic force will charm us *out of* our cares and troubles by insisting that it charms us *into* our cares and troubles and that therein lies its enduring power.

Such a sweeping judgment requires modification, of course, especially for one who dashed off as many pages as Mark Twain did. Much of what he wrote—most of it, in fact—has little power to force us into confronting the deeper aspects of the human situation. Large stretches of the fiction and journalism that he turned out can be exasperating in their excesses and lack of form. But they are seldom dull, and one would have to be weaned on a pickle not to respond at some level to their fanciful charm and exuberant story-telling. Critics have agreed, for the most part, that some of his work is merely entertaining, that some fails completely, but that a select group of titles places Mark Twain among the masters. Of this latter group, there is considerable difference of opinion about the quality of *Pudd'nhead Wilson, Connecticut Yankee, The Mysterious Stranger,* and a few of the shorter pieces. But it is a rare voice indeed that does not acknowledge the supremacy of *Huckleberry Finn.* In this novel, if in no other, his art peaked at a height occupied by the great authors writing in English, his gift as a story-teller fusing perfectly the creation of character and incident with moral implication. It is true that most critics are uncomfortable with the high jinks of the ending, but the dissatisfaction voiced over this vexed section of the novel has usually been directed at correcting adulation rather than calling the merit of the novel into question. Less critical readers seem to accept Tom Sawyer's fantasies about setting Jim free without concerning themselves with the problem of the author's seriousness or the artistic appropriateness of the ending.

The popularity of the novel, as distinct from its critical reputation as high art, is an extraordinary tribute withheld from a considerable number of major literary achievements. One would like to believe that the sheer quality of *Huckleberry Finn* has won over the common reader as he picks his uninstructed way through the literature. Mark Twain's novel still commands a double audience long after its popular readership might have moved on to more recent best-sellers. It has had the advantage, of course, of being one of the few books taught as an American classic in the public schools that is also capable of entertaining for its adventurous incidents alone. And no teacher of literature in the United States can have failed to notice that *Huckleberry Finn* is the American novel most likely to have been read by his foreign students, that Huck and Jim are world figures, not American alone.

In his comprehensive study called *Mark Twain and Huck Finn,* Walter Blair estimated that by 1962 over 10 million copies of *Huckleberry Finn* had been sold in one form or another, three quarters of that figure in the United States and the remainder abroad.[2] There is every reason for believing that the total sales have grown proportionately since then; as it pushed past its seventy-fifth year of publication, Mr. Blair says, it was attracting more readers than ever.[3] *Huckleberry Finn* alone could have made Twain a popular author and a profitable investment for any publisher, but one has only to scan the listings of books in print to be dazzled by the number of other titles by Mark Twain that can be bought everywhere from bookstore shelves to drugstore racks.

There is no adequate accounting for the subtle mixture of qualities that makes *Huckleberry Finn* the popular story that it is, and especially none for the way in which a book that on the surface seems so American, even so parochial in its setting and characters, shimmers with a humanity that transcends its topicality. On one level it is the picaresque adventure of a boy and a slave—an ingenious boy and a comic slave, it is true—each running from his particular bondage. The setting is picturesque: a raft on the river, which Mark Twain describes elsewhere as "the great Mississippi, the majestic, the magnificent Mississippi, rolling its mile-wide tide along." Both on and off the river, he entangles his characters in a varied sequence of incidents involving either their lives or their welfare. All this is gripping enough to make good reading.

Although the story is more colorful and various, it provides narrative interests similar to those in *Tom Sawyer,* which has also retained its high general popularity. The boy, Tom, has become a folk figure of a much more sentimental type than Huck; he is the naughty and imaginative lad who *improves* upon his society's ways instead of escaping them.

Anyone who has read *Tom Sawyer* as a child knows that it is much the same book when he picks it up as an adult. But *Huckleberry Finn* is not; it has grown along with the reader. The raft and the river have

---

[2]Berkeley: University of California Press, 1962. See especially chap. 26, for an account of the sales of the novel around the world.

[3]*Ibid.*, p. 371.

assumed the aura of a better world, the kind we can imagine and hope for but are not likely to inhabit. The characters own in their hearts a moral grandeur that shines through their words, which are often comic and mistaken, and casts their actions into a pantomime of the golden rule: "What you want above all things on a raft is for everybody to be satisfied, and feel right and kind towards the others."

What you want and what you get are seldom the same thing, as Mark Twain well knew, and even what you do may leave much to be desired. Huck's heart is put to severe tests as he and Jim float down the river. The author was too realistic to purify the river and the characters of their baser possibilities, and he smears enough of the mud of real life even there. But mainly it is the life along the banks, in the villages, and on the farms that imposes the ordeals of hypocrisy, selfishness, and custom on the two innocents, forcing them to suffer their way through the journey, to make decisions and take actions with a finely conceived dramatic *agon*.

It was only by accident of birth that Mark Twain knew the river and the people along its banks, all of which were local and peculiar, as much so as in any local color story, but it was genius of language and imagination that transformed them into a narrative convincing us that he had carved out the essence of the American scene. No doubt the author did not know what he was achieving, and if Bernard DeVoto is correct in saying that Mark Twain had found the "true purpose of the book" by setting out to "exhibit the rich variety of life in the great valley"[4] he was consciously only following his profession, which required that he have material for his stories. The subjective experience of reading and the objective record both testify that the novel transcended its materials, and, as Leo Marx has said: "Everyone seems to agree that it is a great book, or even one of the great American books. But we are less certain about what makes it great."[5]

The uncertainty of Mr. Marx's minor premise leaves acres of room for critics to fill in, and at this task they have not been slack. Sophisticated critical analysis of Mark Twain's work, including *Huckleberry Finn*, was somewhat late in developing, much later than general appreciation, but we now have a flood of it. Some of the criticism has been of an order high enough to sharpen our awareness that Mark Twain was more than our most popular writer: he was an artist of the first rank.

The force that Huckleberry Finn's language has exerted on Ameri-

---

[4]*Mark Twain at Work* (Cambridge, Mass.: Harvard University Press, 1942), p. 69.

[5]"Pilot and Passenger: Landscape Conventions and the Style of Huckleberry Finn," *American Literature*, XXVIII (May, 1956), 129.

can writers is well-nigh inestimable, and they have gone hand-in-hand with the critics in praising it and paying their debts. T. S. Eliot spoke for this pervasive influence when he included Mark Twain in his small gallery of English writers who have brought fresh life to their mother tongue:

> Twain, at least in *Huckleberry Finn,* reveals himself to be one of those writers of whom there are not a great many in any literature, who have discovered a new way of writing, valid not only for themselves, but for others. I should place him, in this respect, even with Dryden and Swift, as one of those rare writers who have brought their language up to date and in so doing "purified the dialect of the tribe." In this respect I should place him above Hawthorne.[6]

Eliot spoke as a critic observing the colloquial influence on other writers, one of whom was Faulkner, who observed with appropriately flawed syntax that "Mark Twain is all of our grandfather."[7] It is probably not far amiss to believe that the freedom and informality of written English in general, not only in fiction, has its most influential source in the colloquial style set in motion by Mark Twain when he spoke in the voice of Huck Finn.

Certainly *Huckleberry Finn* is chiefly responsible for raising Mark Twain to the rarefied circle of critical esteem occupied by Melville, Hawthorne, and James.[8] And the respect accorded Melville and Hawthorne is similarly based on single major works, *Moby Dick* and *The Scarlet Letter.* Although Mark Twain's intellectual reputation accounts for the scholarly editions of his work and the steady flow of critical studies, the same respect is paid to other authors, who do not enjoy his popular reputation. His general popularity is nourished by the public's familiarity with his writing rather than by the subtleties of critical examination. In public affection *The Adventures of Tom Sawyer* probably rivals its sequel, and surely the boy Tom, as a folk figure, does. At least as many diners, motels, and advertising agencies have been named after him as after Huck Finn. But the critical reputation of *Tom Sawyer* has

---

[6]"American Literature and the American Language," *Washington University Studies in Language and Literature,* XXIII, n.s. (1935), 16–17.

[7]*Faulkner in the University,* ed. Frederick L. Gwynn and Joseph L. Blotner (New York: Vintage Books, 1959), p. 281.

[8]Among the teachers, scholars, and critics belonging to the Modern Language Association, a 1973 survey shows that these four nineteenth-century Americans—Melville, Hawthorne, James, and Mark Twain—rank among the first twenty-five figures writing in all western languages who are of primary interest. Of twentieth-century Americans, the membership indicated the greatest interest in Faulkner, Eliot, and Hemingway. Heading the list of twenty five are Shakespeare, Chaucer, and Milton.

obliged its defenders to adopt a defensive tone rather than the easy assurance that marks praise for *Huckleberry Finn*.

In the decades since Mark Twain's death critical appraisal has sorted out his work so that a relatively small center remains. The selections in this book discuss, with a few exceptions, those works that are still read with interest and still attract the most critical attention. They represent a wide range of interest in Mark Twain the man, his ideas, and his skills as an artist. The most persistent theme in the criticism focuses on Mark Twain the moralist and social critic and involves his biographical and intellectual experiences, his personality, and his treatment of subject matter.

An extraordinary amount of attention has been paid to Mark Twain's notions of the human situation and for a very good reason: he said so much about it. He seemed to think that both the human situation and the humans who could do nothing about it left nearly everything to be desired, and he voiced these notions with such flair that we are torn between despair at the thoughts and delight with their phrasing. It is hard to believe that the author did not share our ambivalence. Mark Twain was a well-mixed amalgam of literary man and showman, unable to discover any long-term purpose or magnificence in human history, but often enticed by its short term pleasures, almost, it would seem, against his better judgment. Writing about it was one of the pleasures, and how his sentences ring in our ears: "Man is the only animal that blushes. Or needs to"; "Often it does seem such a pity that Noah and his family did not miss the boat." And perhaps he gained an element of control over his own share in human weakness when he reminded us of our debt to Adam, "the first great benefactor of the race. He brought death into the world."

Mark Twain may have lost hope, but he never lost interest. One of his gifts as an artist was his instinctive response to the particular, the immediate, and the concrete, a gift that enabled him to create characters and incidents that were models of individuality. His biographers all record an abundance of exuberance in his reactions to the details of life, whether he was playing a part in home theatricals, cursing King Leopold, or dressing himself in white serge. It always puzzled her, said one of his daughters in a tone she came by honestly, how he "could manage to have an opinion on every incident, accident, invention, or disease in the world."[9] It was her father's good fortune not only to have opinions but to have an audience waiting to relish his every comment.

Pessimism finally became the dominant note in Mark Twain's life,

[9]Quoted in *Mark Twain: Man and Legend,* by DeLancey Ferguson (Indianapolis, Ind.: Bobbs-Merrill, 1943), p. 283.

and it marks his declining years like a flag prominently displayed. His bleak pronouncements, his unfinished fiction, his letters, all display his seemingly settled conviction that human life was a commodity hardly worth the price. His attempts to philosophize in these later days display his tendency to think of human beings as ninepins set in place by an implacable fate only long enough for a cosmic bowling ball to smash them to smithereens. Time and time again, when death struck a dear one, he expressed his feelings by commenting on their good fortune at leaving life. "I always envy the dead," he told his first biographer when his daughter Jean died.[10]

Such sentiment was appropriate for the moment of personal grief and it carries its own logic in Mark Twain's futile contemplation of ultimate human purpose, but if anything is important to remember about this complicated man, it is the well-known fact that he was a bundle of contradictions. Pessimism ran deep in him, but there was also room for other currents to flow. His philosophy was pessimistic, but his temperament was sanguine. And in his writing he expressed a gift for life as intense as his conviction of despair.

[10]Quoted in *Mr. Clemens and Mark Twain,* by Justin Kaplan (New York: Simon and Schuster, 1966), p. 387.

Part I

Biography and General Criticism

Edward Wagenknecht

The Matrix

Samuel Langhorne Clemens was born, the seventh-months child of John Marshall Clemens and Jane Lampton Clemens, in Florida, Monroe County, Missouri, on November 30, 1835.

According to his own belief,[1] he was the third son and fifth child in a family of six. His ancestry was mostly English and partly Irish through Virginia and Kentucky—"Quakers and Indian fighters, independent farmers and small slaveholders," Dixon Wecter[2] calls them. The family liked to speculate about noble ancestors (and a claim on the earlship of Durham), about their kinship with one of King Charles I's judges, and even about a strain of Spanish blood supposed to have been brought into the family by an ambassadorial Clemens. However all this may have been in fact, it importantly stimulated Mark Twain's imagination and furnished him literary material—certainly in *The American Claimant,* perhaps also, much more importantly, in connection with the Duke and the Dauphin in *Huckleberry Finn.*

When Samuel was four years old, the family removed to Hannibal, in Marion County, on the west bank of the Mississippi.

"Circled with bluffs" and "the shining river in the

---

[1]Samuel C. Webster *(Mark Twain, Business Man,* [Boston: Little, Brown, 1946] 44), who descends from Mark Twain's sister Pamela, claims that there was yet another child, Pleasants Hannibal, who died at the age of three months, before Mark Twain was born. This fact, if it is a fact, Mark Twain never knew, and when Webster mentioned it to him, he refused to accept it.

[2]Much the best account of Mark Twain's ancestors is in Dixon Wecter, *Sam Clemens of Hannibal,* chaps. I–II (Boston: Houghton Mifflin, 1952).

From Mark Twain: The Man and His Work, *by Edward Wagenknecht. Revised Edition copyright 1961 by the University of Oklahoma Press. Third Edition copyright 1967 by the University of Oklahoma Press.*

foreground"[3]—the river that was the highway of the nation, the river whose great historian he was to become—Hannibal, on its physical side, became, in *Tom Sawyer* and in *Huckleberry Finn,* a part of the literature of the world. Mark Twain gave us the Missouri countryside also, notably in those magnificent passages in his autobiography in which he describes his summers on his Uncle John Quarles's farm, near Florida. Not even "The Eve of St. Agnes" is richer in sense-impressions than those descriptions.

There were only 450 people in Hannibal when Mark Twain came there, but it held 3,000 and was the second city in the state by the time he left. Though it was rude enough even in Mark Twain's idealized memory of it, it was not quite the cultural wilderness it has sometimes been represented. A good many of its families, like Mark Twain's own, had come from the South, and they brought something of tradition and background with them. Carriages, wagons, omnibuses, river boats, and flour were manufactured in Hannibal. The Marion Female Academy was housed in the Christian church, and the Reverend Daniel Emerson's English and Classical School held its sessions in the First Presbyterian church. There were five newspapers, three bookstores, and a public library in which Mark Twain's older brother Orion was a shareholder. Hannibal papers advertised the better British and American magazines, and newspaper "fillers" drew freely upon the classics and upon standard English writers, particularly of the eighteenth century.[4]

Little sympathy existed at any time between Mark Twain and his father. The boy's volatile temperament apparently lay beyond the range of the father's understanding, as also, in all likelihood, did that of the mother from whom he inherited it. John Marshall Clemens was an austere man, in religion a freethinker, in ethical conduct an undeviating puritan, a lawyer by profession, a merchant by necessity, an unselfish leader in all community enterprises. In all likelihood, Mark Twain owed more to him than he ever realized. Mark's almost fanatical financial rectitude was that of John Marshall Clemens all over again; so was the element of stability in his complex character which, with his genius, differentiated him from his lovable but impractical brother Orion. It would be interesting to know to what extent, if any, his religious apostasy was influenced by his father's example. When he was dying, John Marshall Clemens was asked by a clergyman whether he believed in Christ and in the saving blood of Christ; he answered, "I do." The son died without benefit of clergy, but he is reported to have pressed his daughter's hand and murmured, "Good-by, dear, if we meet——." Even

---

[3]Albert Bigelow Paine, *Mark Twain: A Biography,* I (New York: Harper and Bros., 1912), 26.

[4]See Minnie M. Brashear, *Mark Twain, Son of Missouri,* especially chap. II (Chapel Hill: The University of North Carolina Press, 1934).

in minor matters there are resemblances between the two. The father, also, was absentminded, and he anticipated Mark's interest in inventions within his limited means when he tinkered with a perpetual motion machine.

With the mother the case was very different. Her temperament was Mark Twain's temperament, and her influence upon him can be seen at every turn. It was not at all the narrowing influence which some writers have described. Jane Lampton Clemens was a Presbyterian, but she was not a fanatic, and her religion was never a burden to her. She was an intensely social being—in her youth a Kentucky belle devoted to dancing. She loved the theater and hated housekeeping. At one period she smoked a pipe.

From her Mark Twain inherited many specific tastes and tendencies—his love of red, his tenderness toward all animals, especially cats, his quick, impulsive emotion, his lifelong habit of protecting the outcast and unfortunate. No stray animal was ever turned away from Jane Clemens's door. At one time she was feeding nineteen cats. But she kept no birds, for she could not endure to think of any creature deprived of its freedom.

She had her son's curiosity also. With her it took the special form of investigating strange religions, which she considered carefully but without committing herself to them. She was capable of great indignation and of dauntless courage. Once she opened her door to a fugitive girl whom her brutal father was pursuing with a rope, then planted herself in it and gave the brute such a tongue-lashing that he slunk away. Like her son, she mingled freely, in her conversation, fact and fiction. Like him, she was unconventional, as when she heard two men on a train arguing about where Mark Twain was born and turned around and told them. "I'm his mother," she said. "I ought to know. I was there." Something of his cryptic gift of phrase was hers also, as shown in her remark, "Never learn to do anything. If you don't learn, you'll always find someone else to do it for you."

John Marshall Clemens died in 1847. It was Mark Twain's impression in later life that he was immediately taken out of school and apprenticed to the printing trade. It has now been shown that he remained in school at least until 1849, though he probably worked part time as many schoolboys have done.[5] This was at first in Hannibal, for his brother and others, but from June, 1853, on, elsewhere. He tarried in Washington, Philadelphia, and New York. He worked again for Orion in Keokuk, Iowa, stayed for a little while in Cincinnati, then, according to the established story, set out for South America to earn his fortune. But we now know that he did not wait until he got to New

[5]See Wecter, *Sam Clemens of Hannibal*, 131.

Orleans to decide instead to apprentice himself to Horace Bixby and learn piloting on the Mississippi.[6] Indeed a notebook entry shows that this glamorous profession had already appealed to him as early as 1855, when he was nineteen.[7]

To become a pilot, Mark Twain set himself "the stupendous task of learning the twelve hundred miles of the Mississippi River between St. Louis and New Orleans—of knowing it as exactly and unfailingly, even in the dark, as one knows the way to his own features." The river absorbed his energies from 1857 until the coming of the Civil War in 1861, and this period has a glamour all its own in his life, for this was when he established his independence and proved to himself and to others that he was able to do a man's work in the world. "When I find a well-drawn character in fiction or biography," he was to write in later years, "I generally take a warm personal interest in him, for the reason that I have known him before—met him on the river." Yet he may have exaggerated the importance of the Mississippi period, for the more we learn of his Hannibal and Keokuk days, the more deeply do his roots seem to sink into that soil. Nostalgia informs *Life on the Mississippi*, and the pathos of distance hovers about it. The coarser, harsher aspects of steamboat life, in an age of cutthroat competition and easy indulgences, are passed over altogether; a tired man is trying to recapture his lost youth.

Some students of Mark Twain have been of the opinion that it was as a pilot that he really found himself, adjusting himself to life, experiencing a satisfaction which not even his later trade of authorship could ever give him. There are times when Mark Twain himself supports this opinion. "I am a person who would quit authorizing in a minute to go to piloting," he wrote Howells in 1874, "if the madam would stand it." But he is writing under the spell of the enthusiasm awakened by going back to the river, in his imagination, for his Mississippi articles: it is authorship that has inspired him even while he disclaims interest in authorship! He might have returned to piloting after the war if he had cared to do so; there was no "madam" to hold him then. Mining did not really suit him, but when he gave it up, he went on to journalism, not back to steamboating. The truth is that the pilot's life, though ideally suited to Mark Twain's needs at a critical period in his development, could never have absorbed him permanently. In his old age he used to have nightmares in which he was haunted by the horror of being obliged to go back to the river for bread.

It was during his pilot days, too, that Mark Twain experienced the

[6]Walter Blair, *Mark Twain and "Huck Finn,"* (Berkeley: The University of California Press, 1960), p. 41.

[7]Edwin H. Carpenter, Jr., *Mark Twain . . .* , (San Marino: The Huntington Library, 1947), p. 11.

first great sorrow of his life. In 1858 his younger brother Henry, drawn to the river by Sam's success, lost his life as the result of injuries sustained in the horrible *Pennsylvania* steamboat disaster. A contemporary newspaper reported that when Sam arrived at the bedside of his injured brother, "his feelings so much overcame him, at the scalded and emaciated form before him, that he sank to the floor overpowered."[8] It was the first of many disasters for which his "trained Presbyterian conscience" was to cause him to blame himself.

Mark Twain's connection with the Civil War was both brief and loose. He may have had some military connection in New Orleans; if so, we know none of the details.[9] Nor do we know a great deal more about his adventures with an informally organized Confederate group in Missouri, for "The Private History of a Campaign That Failed" mingles fact with fiction. Nevertheless the fact remains that Lieutenant Clemens shortly mustered himself out of Confederate service and went to Nevada with his brother Orion, a staunch Union man, whom President Lincoln had appointed secretary of the Territory.

The journey is described in *Roughing It*. In Nevada, Mark Twain entered upon his various mining activities and came in contact with many different aspects of Western life. He had drifted to Aurora, California, and was poor indeed in this world's goods when the opportunity came, late in the summer of 1862, to take a place on the staff of the Virginia City (Nevada) *Enterprise,* a paper edited by Joe Goodman in an atmosphere of frontier irresponsibility and bohemian camaraderie, flavored with a good deal in the way of sound literary taste and judgment. Here he first used the name Mark Twain.[10] and here he began to build up his West Coast reputation. In those days the journalistic hoax was still his favorite form of humor, and the consequences were not always pleasant. The results of one affair involved a precipitate retreat to San Francisco, where he found a somewhat uncongenial berth on the *Morning Call*.[11] From San Francisco, too, he found it prudent in time to

[8]Quoted by Fred W. Lorch, "Mark Twain and the *Pennsylvania* Disaster," *Twainian,* vol. IX, (Jan.–Feb., 1950), p. 2.

[9]See Ernest E. Leisy, ed., *The Letters of Quintus Curtius Snodgrass,* (Dallas: Southern Methodist University Press, 1946), ix.

[10]"Mark Twain" is a piloting term and means two fathoms or "safe water." Samuel Clemens was afterwards under the impression that he had borrowed it from the nearly illiterate Captain Isaiah Sellers, and Paine accepted his statement, but it now seems as though this were one more example of his remembering the thing that did not happen. See Ernest E. Leisy, "Mark Twain and Isaiah Sellers," *American Literature,* vol. XIII, (1942), 398–404; George Hiram Brownell, "A Question as to the Origin of the Name 'Mark Twain'," *Twainian,* n.s. vol. I, (Feb., 1942), pp. 4–7, and cf. April, pp. 7–8 and May, pp. 3–5.

[11]For the hoaxes and other difficulties which contributed to Mark Twain's departure from Virginia City (and which are not always accurately related), see, especially, Henry Nash Smith and Frederick Anderson, eds., *Mark Twain of the "Enterprise"* (Berkeley:

retreat, but this time the circumstances were all to his credit. He had been too frank in his criticism of a corrupt police department. For three months he lived in Calaveras County, where, with Jim Gillis, he tried pocket mining on Jackass Hill. In 1865, Artemus Ward, whom Mark Twain had met briefly in Virginia City, wrote from the East coast to ask for a sketch to be included in a new book of humor. Mark Twain sent a story he had heard about a jumping frog. Arriving too late to be included in the book, "Jim Smiley and His Jumping Frog," as it was then called, appeared instead in the *Saturday Press,* on November 18, 1865; this marks the real beginning of Mark Twain's Eastern reputation.[12]

In 1866 the Sacramento *Union* sent Mark Twain to the Sandwich (or, as we now call them, the Hawaiian) Islands; while there he brought his paper a "scoop" in the form of an interview with the survivors of the *Hornet* disaster, in which interest was very keen at the time. His initial contribution to *Harper's Magazine* dealt with the same subject, but unfortunately his name appeared as "Mark Swain." In December, 1866, he went east, as he supposed, for a visit. Unexpectedly, he lectured at Cooper Union. Still more unexpectedly, he sailed, in June, 1867, on the *Quaker City* Mediterranean steamboat excursion for Europe and the Holy Land, writing, for the *Alta California* and other papers, the travel letters which, revised in *The Innocents Abroad,* were soon to make him the most famous humorist of his time. It was indeed a momentous voyage, for both his personal and his professional future were decided by it. One day, in the Bay of Smyrna, a wealthy young man of Elmira, New York, named Charles J. Langdon, showed him a miniature reproduction of the face of his sister Olivia. With that face Mark Twain immediately fell hopelessly and everlastingly in love. In July, 1869, *The Innocents Abroad* was published, and on February 2, 1870, Samuel L. Clemens and Olivia Langdon were married.

Successful as *The Innocents Abroad* had been, it had not yet occurred to Mark Twain that he could rely for his livelihood upon authorship alone; he bought, therefore, an interest in the Buffalo *Express.* This venture did not turn out well. The first months of marriage were almost fantastically overshadowed by sickness. In August, Mrs. Clemens's father died, and on November 7, after Livy had been cruelly jolted in a

The University of California Press, 1957) and DeLancey Ferguson, " 'The Petrified Truth,' " *Colophon,* n.s. vol. II, no. 2 (1937), 189–196.

[12]*Jim Smiley and His Jumping Frog* may be read, with an introduction by Franklin J. Meine, in a little book published in Chicago by the Pocahontas Press in 1940. It was not Sam Clemens's first story or even his first appearance in the East. "The Dandy Frightening the Squatter" was published in the Boston *Carpet Bag,* May 1, 1852, when he was only sixteen years old. This tale was discovered by Mr. Meine. For Sam's cub-printer writings in the Hannibal *Journal,* when Orion injudiciously left him in charge, see Brashear, *Mark Twain, Son of Missouri,* chap. IV.

cab, her first child, Langdon, was prematurely born. By the end of 1871, the Clemenses had moved to the Nook Farm neighborhood in Hartford, Connecticut, where, in 1874, Mark Twain was to build on Farmington Avenue the beautiful "English violet" house, which, now happily open to the public, is still one of the rococo show places of the Western world. In Hartford, in 1872, little Langdon died, and in the same year *Roughing It* was published.

The years 1872 and 1873 were spent largely in England, lecturing, being entertained, and laying the foundations of a later world fame. During the Hartford years the summer months were spent at Quarry Farm, near Elmira, the home of Mrs. Clemens's sister, and here, in an open-air hilltop study, much of Mark Twain's best writing was done. During these years, again, Mark Twain became the happy father of three little girls—Susy, Clara, and Jean; he also extended his business interests, developing the tendency toward unwise investments that led finally to his business collapse. In 1873 he published, with Charles Dudley Warner, a Hartford neighbor, his first extended piece of fiction, *The Gilded Age*. In 1876 came *The Adventures of Tom Sawyer*. A trip to Europe yielded *A Tramp Abroad* in 1880. *The Prince and the Pauper,* a serious historical juvenile came out in 1881. In 1883 *Life on the Mississippi* appeared, to be followed a year later by *Adventures of Huckleberry Finn*. In 1889 came an earnest, extended satire, *A Connecticut Yankee in King Arthur's Court*.

In 1891, harassed by financial difficulties, Clemens closed his Hartford house and moved with his family to Europe. A long struggle ended in 1894 when the failure of both the Paige typesetter and the Charles L. Webster publishing company left Mark Twain nearly $100,000 in debt. Like Sir Walter Scott before him, he refused to take advantage of the bankruptcy laws and set out in the summer of 1895, in the company of Mrs. Clemens and their second daughter, Clara, for a lecture tour of the world. Opening in Cleveland, he gave twenty-four midsummer lectures in the United States before sailing across the Pacific from Vancouver, B. C. His success was all that could have been hoped for—even in India and Ceylon the response was enthusiastic —but just as the burden of debt had been lifted, Susy, Mark Twain's eldest daughter, whom he so passionately loved, and who had inherited so much of his own great spirit, died suddenly, across the ocean from him in Hartford, and half the reawakening glory of life died with her.

The books continued—*The American Claimant,* his least effective long story, in 1891; *Tom Sawyer Abroad* and *Pudd'nhead Wilson,* both partial successes, in 1894; then, in 1896, both *Tom Sawyer, Detective* and a long, serious historical novel, *Personal Recollections of Joan of Arc,* which was written for love and serialized without his name in

Harper's Magazine, because he wanted it to be judged on its own merits. *Following the Equator,* his last travel book, came along in 1897, to tell the story of the world tour and pay off the last of his debts.

The Clemens family remained in Europe until 1900, when they returned to America, though not to Hartford, for Mrs. Clemens felt she could never bear to see the Hartford house again. In 1903, when her health finally broke, they removed to Florence, and it was here, in an old Italian villa, on June 5, 1904, that the much-loved Livy died. Feeling singularly helpless without her, Mark Twain and his two remaining daughters brought her body and their possessions and themselves back to America; with characteristic thoughtfulness, President Theodore Roosevelt personally ordered that they be extended the courtesy of the Port of New York.

They took a house on lower Fifth Avenue, and Mark Twain resumed his writing. He wrote enormously during the last years of his life, but much of what he wrote remained unfinished and unpublished. Mrs. Clemens had always opposed the publication of his "gospel" of determinism, *What Is Man?.* It was privately printed, unsigned, in 1906, but it was not added to his collected works until 1917. *The Mysterious Stranger,* his last important work of fiction, was published in a special format, with illustrations by N. C. Wyeth which Mark Twain would have loved, in 1916. The last books—all brief, all save the second quite unimportant—that their author himself saw through the press were *Christian Science* and *Extract from Captain Stormfield's Visit to Heaven,* [13] both in 1907, and *Is Shakespeare Dead?* in 1909. Yet he was always writing, always when he was not playing billiards, or cursing the warlords, or playing with cats and little girls. He filled the magazines, and he filled the public eye. The reporters were after him continually; no public occasion was complete without him. A series of academic honors was climaxed wonderfully in 1907 when Oxford University draped his venerable whiteness with the scarlet robes of a Doctor of Letters. In 1908 he moved to his beautiful new house, "Stormfield," at Redding, Connecticut. On the day before Christmas, 1909, life struck at him for the last time, when his youngest daughter, Jean, was taken with an epileptic seizure and died in her bath. Halley's Comet had blazed in the skies just before Mark Twain was born in 1835. It was due back in 1910, and he had said he would go out with it. It reached its maximum splendor on April 19. On April 21, Mark Twain quietly died.

---

[13]*Captain Stormfield* is an early work, but for some reason Mark Twain always considered it very shocking. The full text was not printed until *Report from Paradise* appeared in 1952.

Jay B. Hubbell

Mark Twain

American writers were slow to learn to write like Americans. The spell of English literature was too strong. Hawthorne, for instance, was an accomplished stylist, but for our taste today he wrote too much like nineteenth-century Englishmen. Emerson had a fondness for the earthy talk of teamsters and farmers, but his essays are too reminiscent of the rhetoric of the lyceum lecturer and the Unitarian minister. Lowell in *The Biglow Papers* was the earliest of our eminent men of letters to make effective use of the New England dialect; but the first notable humorists to write in dialect were newspapermen: Seba Smith, who wrote the "Jack Downing" letters from Maine, and Augustus Baldwin Longstreet, the author of *Georgia Scenes*. Our various regional dialects, whether southern, western, or New England, do not vary greatly from one another. In the aggregate they represent the speech of uneducated Americans of the backwoods in all sections; they are the basis of what in the twentieth century H. L. Mencken was to call "the American Language."

The southern and western humorists were men of some education, most of whom came from states to the east or the north. They were fascinated by the speech and the behavior of those whom they encountered in the semi-frontier regions of the South and the West: adventurers, braggarts, gamblers, fools and rascals, sharpers and their victims, tellers of tall tales, and notable hunters and scouts like David Crockett and Daniel Boone. Among the legendary characters that figure in their tales are Mike Fink, King of the Keelboatmen; Simon Suggs, who robs a congregation at a camp meeting; and Ransy Sniffle, the Georgia

From Jay B. Hubbell, Who are the Major American Writers? *Reprinted by permission of the publisher. Copyright, 1972 by Duke University Press, Durham, North Carolina.*

victim of hookworm who never comes fully alive except when he is fomenting or witnessing a fight. Some of the humorists were themselves accomplished raconteurs, and no doubt many of the tales they wrote out for publication had already been shaped as they were told to eager listeners. Even in their written form, the oral tradition is still strong. These humorous sketches and tales were written not for backwoodsmen but for more sophisticated readers on the Atlantic seaboard. The humorists were in a sense pioneer realists and local colorists, forerunners of Joel Chandler Harris and Mark Twain; and like them they often satirized the sentimental, the romantic, and the bombastic.

Most of our best-known writers of the early nineteenth century had no high regard for any humorists except Lowell and Holmes, Brahmins from the neighborhood of Boston. There was, however, a Yankee from Vermont who had a different idea. William Trotter Porter (1809–1858), who had spent much time in the South, was editor of the *Spirit of the Times,* a sporting magazine in which many of the best southern humorous sketches first appeared. Porter reprinted some of the best pieces in two collections: *The Big Bear of Arkansas* (1845) and *A Quarter Race in Kentucky* (1846). In the preface to the earlier collection he announced: ''A new vein of literature, as original as it is inexhaustible in its source, has been opened in this country within a very few years.'' Though Thomas Bailey Aldrich and Edmund Clarence Stedman thought otherwise, Porter confidently asserted that the newspaper humorists had ''conferred signal honor on the rising literature of America.''

The sketches of the humorists, first appearing in one newspaper, were quickly copied in many another news sheet. In his boyhood Samuel Langhorne Clemens (1835–1910) no doubt read many of them—in addition to literature of a more respectable sort—and probably set some of them in type for his brother Orion's paper, the Hannibal *Journal.* The first of his writings to attract wide attention was ''The Jumping Frog of Calaveras County,'' which he wrote out to please Artemus Ward. The manuscript arrived in New York too late to be included in Ward's book; but when it was printed in the *Saturday Press* on November 18, 1865, it was copied far and wide. Mark Twain thus got his first taste of nationwide fame, but that was not the kind of reputation that he wanted. On January 20, 1866, he wrote to his mother and sister expressing disappointment that the New York people should single out a ''villainous backwoods sketch'' which he had written only because Artemus Ward had asked for it. He thought more highly of articles that in 1864 and 1865 he had printed in the *Californian,* which seemed to him ''the best literary weekly in the United States.'' Bret Harte, who also wrote for the *Californian,* on November 10, 1866, wrote in the Springfield, Massachusetts, *Republican:*

He [Mark Twain] has shrewdness and a certain hearty abhor[r]ence of shams which will make his faculty serviceable to mankind. His talent is so well based that he can write seriously and well when he chooses, which is perhaps the best test of true humor. His faults are crudeness, coarseness, and an occasional Panurge-like plainness of statement. I am particular in these details, for I believe he deserves this space and criticism, and I think I recognize a new star rising in this western horizon.

Innocents Abroad (1869) was a popular success, but few besides Howells and Harte praised it for its literary qualities. The New York *Nation* made no mention of its literary merits, and Josiah Gilbert Holland called its author a "mere fun-maker of ephemeral popularity."

In 1870, after Mark Twain married Olivia Langdon and became part-owner of the Buffalo *Express*, he still saw himself as a newspaper-man and a humorous lecturer rather than a man of letters. In 1872 he published *Roughing It* and settled in Hartford, Connecticut. In the following year appeared *The Gilded Age,* a novel that he had written in collaboration with his new neighbor, Charles Dudley Warner, a well-known man of letters. Mark Twain was now discovering his true métier in fiction. In *The Adventures of Tom Sawyer* (1876) he began to exploit his richest mine of literary materials, the memories of his youth. Born in Missouri of southern parents, he had spent his formative years in the western South; and he found that what he remembered of his life in the Mississippi River country served him better than his recollections of California and Nevada. With his journalistic training Mark Twain was always sensitive to changes in literary fashions which affected his market, and in the early eighties he could not fail to note the extraordinary popularity of stories of the Old South. Indeed, some of the best of them were being written by two of his friends, George W. Cable and Joel Chandler Harris. There are no more memorable descriptions of Southern life than those in *Huckleberry Finn* and the earlier chapters of *Life on the Mississippi.* The life of the Old South that Mark Twain knew was more primitive than that portrayed in Thomas Nelson Page's *In Ole Virginia,* but the South that he knew was not frontier country. The American frontier had passed on westward by the time Mark Twain was born.

Memorable also are some of the scenes in *Pudd'nhead Wilson* (1895), in which belatedly Mark Twain returned to the southern scene. Before that time, however, the vogue of southern stories had waned; and there was under way a revival of historical romance led by Robert Louis Stevenson. Mark Twain had made use of a romantic period in English history in *The Prince and the Pauper* (1882). *Joan of Arc,* which for a time he considered his best book, came in 1896. A better book was the satiric *A Connecticut Yankee in King Arthur's Court* (1889), a favorite with Howells and Stedman. He lived on until 1910, but apart from *The Mysterious Stranger* and "The Man That Corrupted Hadleyburg," his later published writings have little importance.

In its issue of October, 1898, the *Critic* asked: "Who are the four most famous of living authors?" and in answer to its own query named Tolstoy, Zola, Ruskin, and Mark Twain. It is true nevertheless, as Howells maintained in his *My Mark Twain* (1910), that in his own country "polite learning [had] hesitated his praise."

> In proportion as people thought themselves refined they questioned that quality which all recognize in him now. . . . I went' with him to see Longfellow, but I do not think Longfellow made much of him, and Lowell made less. . . . It was two of my most fastidious Cambridge friends who accepted him with the English, the European entirely—namely, Charles Eliot Norton and Professor Francis J. Child.

Until after the end of the century few of the literary historians recognized Mark Twain as a major American writer. Richardson and Beers failed to see that he was any more important than Josh Billings and Petroleum V. Nasby. Even W. P. Trent, who was among the first scholars to see the importance of the western and southern humorists, could not in 1903 rank Mark Twain as the equal of those Cambridge humorists, Lowell and Holmes; and he regarded the author of *Joan of Arc* as greatly inferior to Scott as a historical romancer. Mark Twain is not included in William Crary Brownell's *American Prose Masters* (1909) or John Erskine's *Leading American Novelists* (1910), and there are no selections from his works in Norman Foerster's *The Chief American Prose Writers* (1916).

In 1900, however, Professor Walter Bronson of Brown University had ranked Twain as the "greatest writer of the West," greater he felt than Bret Harte. "Time," he said, "will winnow much chaff from his pages, but much of great merit will remain." In 1900 also Professor Barrett Wendell of Harvard wrote that "in certain moods one is disposed for all its eccentricity to call [*Huckleberry Finn*] the most admirable work of literary art as yet produced on this continent." In 1904 Professor Richard Burton wrote that the United States possessed "one living writer of indisputable genius . . . Mark Twain." Professor William Lyon Phelps of Yale was also among the first scholars to praise Mark Twain as a major American writer. Before Mark Twain's death in 1910 three universities had bestowed honorary degrees upon him: Yale in 1901, Missouri in 1902, and Oxford in 1907. In 1915 Fred Lewis Pattee in *A History of American Literature since 1870* wrote: "His generation bought his books for the fun in them; their children are finding now that their fathers bought not, as they supposed, clownish ephemera, but true literature, the classics of the period." In 1921 Stuart P. Sherman's chapter in *The Cambridge History* seemed to give official sanction to Mark Twain's rank as a great American writer, and in the same year Carl Van Doren in *The American Novel* gave it as his opinion that the two greatest American novels were *The Scarlet Letter* and *Huckleberry Finn*.

One of the first American critics to see Mark Twain as a major writer was a professor of English at Columbia University, but it is perhaps well to remember that it was not until his fortieth year that Brander Matthews (1852-1929) began his distinguished career at Columbia University. He had tried his hand at writing verse, fiction, and literary and dramatic criticism; and he had spent many months in France and England. He was not only a great teacher but a man of letters as well. In his "Memories of Mark Twain" (in *The Tocsin of Revolt,* 1922) he recalled that he had read "The Jumping Frog" story at the age of fifteen and from that time on he had followed Mark Twain's literary career with keen interest. He recalled also that soon after its publication he had "had the pleasure of reviewing [*Huckleberry Finn*] for the London *Saturday Review,* hailing it as one of the masterpieces of American fiction."

For the Uniform Edition of Mark Twain's writings in 1899 Brander Matthews wrote an introductory essay entitled "Biographical Criticism" (reprinted later as "An Appreciation"). Mark Twain, he noted, had "ripened in knowledge and power since he first attracted attention as a wild Western funny man." And yet, he added, "In many of the discussions of American literature he is dismissed as though he were only a competitor of his predecessors, Artemus Ward and John Phoenix, instead of being what he is really, a writer who is to be classed—at whatever interval only time may decide—rather with Cervantes and Molière." Mark Twain's best books, Matthews felt sure, were not those with romantic European historical backgrounds but those which dealt with the life the author knew at first hand in the Mississippi River country. *Huckleberry Finn,* he said, is "the finest of his books, the deepest in its insight, and the widest in its appeal." It is, he asserted, "very much more than a funny book, it is a marvelously accurate portrayal of a whole civilization." "No American author," he added, "has at his command a style more nervous, more varied, more flexible, or more various than Mark Twain's. His colloquial style," he continued, "should not hide from us his mastery of all the devices of rhetoric."

Consider the tale of the Blue Jay in "A Tramp Abroad," wherein the humor is sustained by unstated pathos; what could be better told than this, with every word the right word and in the right place? And take Huck Finn's description of the storm when he was alone on the island, which is in dialect, which will not parse, which bristles with double negatives, but which none the less is one of the finest passages of descriptive prose in all American literature.

Huckleberry Finn was a great popular success, but there is scant evidence to show that American literary critics recognized it as a masterpiece. Like other books sold by subscription, this novel was not widely reviewed. The *Century Magazine,* however, assigned it to a very competent reviewer, Thomas Sergeant Perry, who saw that it was a much greater book than *Tom Sawyer.* Perry was a native of New England, but the book drew more unfavorable criticism from that section than from any other. The Concord, Massachusetts, library banned the book as "rough, coarse, and inelegant, dealing with a series of experiences not elevating. . . . It is the veriest trash." In Boston both the daily *Transcript* and the weekly *Literary World* approved the verdict of the Concord library committee. In Springfield the *Republican* branded the book as "trashy and vicious."

> The trouble with Mr. Clemens is that he has no reliable sense of propriety. His notorious speech at an *Atlantic* dinner, marshalling Longfellow and Emerson and Whittier [Holmes] in vulgar parodies in a Western miner's cabin, illustrates this, but not in much more relief than the "Adventures of Tom Sawyer" did, or these Huckleberry Finn stories do. . . . They are no better in tone than the dime novels which flood the blood-and-thunder reading population.

Professor Arthur L. Vogelback, who quoted this passage in his study of the reception of *Huckleberry Finn (American Literature,* November, 1939), concluded:

> In these indignant comments, it is, of course, easy to identify the genteel tradition. Critics who used such words as "vulgar," "coarse," "inelegant," in condemning the books, indicated by implication the qualities they deemed necessary to literature—"refinement," "delicacy," and "elegance."

One thinks of a Pudd'nhead Wilson epigram that Mark Twain inserted in *Following the Equator* (1897): "There are no people who are quite so vulgar as the over-refined ones."

Among men of letters in England and America there were a few who publicly recognized *Huckleberry Finn* as a contemporary classic. Conspicuous among them was William Dean Howells. That small number, however, does not include Matthew Arnold, for whom Mark Twain was only a vulgar funny man, or Henry James, who regarded him as a writer for immature minds. Joel Chandler Harris, who in 1908 was to refer to Mark Twain as "not only our greatest humorist but our greatest writer of fiction," in November, 1885, wrote in the *Critic* that "there is not in our fictive literature a more wholesome book than 'Huckleberry Finn.' " It teaches, he added "the lesson of honesty, justice, mercy." After reading these words in the *Critic,* Mark Twain wrote to thank Harris for "the good word about Huck, that abused child of mine, who has had so much mud flung at him."

In England in 1883, before the publication of *Huckleberry Finn,* Thomas Hardy had asked Howells: "Why don't people [in America] understand that Mark Twain is not merely a great humorist?"[1] On August 3, 1886, Brander Matthews had a talk with Robert Louis Stevenson which he briefly described in *These Many Years* (1917): "What I remember most vividly was the high appreciation of 'Huckleberry Finn' that he expressed, calling it a far finer work artistically than 'Tom Sawyer,' partly because it was a richer book morally; and he wound up by declaring it to be the most important addition to the fiction of our language that had been made for ten years." Andrew Lang, though he said he would not read *A Connecticut Yankee,* praised *Huckleberry Finn* in the *Critic* for July 25, 1891, as "a nearly flawless gem of romance and humor." Bernard Shaw had praise for Mark Twain's books. Rudyard Kipling, on his first visit to the United States, went out of his way to see Mark Twain. A decade later he wrote to his American publisher, Frank Doubleday: "He [Mark Twain] is the biggest man you have on your side of the water by a damn sight, and don't you forget it. Cervantes was a relation of his."

In 1920 when Mark Twain was elected to the Hall of Fame for Great Americans, his status as a major American writer seemed assured. The college of electors, however, had not reckoned with the young intellectuals who were now systematically denigrating the standard British and American authors of the nineteenth century. It was in 1920 that one of the ablest of the young literary radicals launched a devastating attack in *The Ordeal of Mark Twain.* Van Wyck Brooks saw in Mark Twain one of the most gifted of all American writers, one

---

[1] A year earlier Professor John Nichol of the University of Glasgow in his book on *American Literature* had asserted that Mark Twain had done "perhaps more than any other living writer to lower the literary tone of English speaking people."

who might have developed into a great satirist like Swift or Cervantes. Brooks, whose appreciation of humor in literature was rather weak, was a social rather than an aesthetic critic, and he looked to American writers to take the lead in bringing about a transformed social and economic order. He saw in Mark Twain the victim of a society that failed to stimulate and nourish its geniuses.

The three persons who in Brooks's view were most to be blamed for Mark Twain's failure were his mother, his wife, and his friend and adviser, William Dean Howells. Of his mother Brooks wrote: "Jane Clemens, in short, was the embodiment of that old-fashioned, cast-iron Calvinism which had proved so favorable to the life of enterprising action but which perceived the scent of the devil in any least expression of what is now known as the creative impulse." Olivia Langdon, argued Brooks, did her best to make of her husband not a great writer but a gentleman and a money-maker. Said Brooks: "From the moment of his marriage his artistic integrity, already compromised, had, as a matter of fact, been irreparably destroyed. . . ." Brooks in 1920 had not discovered how wrong he was when he wrote of Howells: "He [Mark Twain], this divided soul, had sought the great leader and had found only an irresponsible child like himself, a child who told him that you had to sneak off behind the barn if you wanted to smoke the pipe of truth."

The indictment was a formidable one. Brooks had ransacked Mark Twain's books and published letters and Paine's huge biography, and with great skill he had marshaled numerous details in support of his thesis. He explained the pessimism and cynicism which are so conspicuous in Mark Twain's later writings and conversation: "That bitterness of his was the effect of a certain miscarriage in his creative life, a balked personality, and arrested development . . . which for him destroyed the meaning of life." In the 1935 edition of *The Ordeal* Brooks was less sharply critical of Mark Twain.

Brooks's book caused critics and scholars to take sides in a debate that continued intermittently for years. Various scholars brought forth convincing evidence that Brooks's vivid portraits of Mark Twain's mother and wife were distorted and inaccurate. As to Brooks's thesis that Mark Twain could not in an American environment become the great literary leader that Brooks had hoped for, Clarence Gohdes's comment is not irrelevant: "As a thinker, Mark Twain is too inconsistent and too shallow to be of much importance."

The most persistent of Brooks's critics was Bernard De Voto, who in 1938 became custodian of the Mark Twain Papers. He pointed out various errors in Brooks's indictment and gave his own interpretation of

Mark Twain's significance: "Mark Twain was a frontier humorist. His literary intelligence was shaped by the life of the frontier and found expression in the themes and forms developed by the humor of the frontier." De Voto, himself a product of the West, chose to make little of Mark Twain's southern background and to ignore the fact that Mark Twain had had no experience of frontier life until he was twenty-six years old. De Voto would not have agreed with Fred Lewis Pattee, who in a book of selections from Mark Twain's writings wrote in 1935: "The Mark Twain that has endured was born in New England. He needed restraint, literary ideals, suggestion, and publication in adequate magazines." "What," said Pattee, "would he have written had he remained in San Francisco?"

DeLancey Ferguson, after a study of revisions in the manuscript of *Huckleberry Finn*, concluded that whether made by Mark or Livy the revisions "are not the dilution of grim realism to make it meat for babies; they are the work of a skilled craftsman removing the unessential, adding vividness to dialogue and description, and smoothing incongruities." Mark Twain, he concluded, was not a folk humorist but a highly skilled man of letters.

Too much has been made of the pessimism of the aging Mark Twain, and we do not need to go to the Freudians for an explanation of it. How indeed could any one expect important results to come from the application, by an amateur like Brooks, of Freudian methods to a writer who could not be questioned or examined by a competent physician? Mark Twain was deeply grieved by the deaths of those he loved most: a son, two daughters, and his beloved wife. There was in addition a business failure followed by bankruptcy and the need once again to return to the lecture platform that he had come to hate. Not to be overlooked also are his declining health and energy and frustrations concerning his later writings. The world in which he spent the last decades of his long life was immeasurably remote from the world in which he had grown up; and neither his own country nor the rest of the civilized world was fulfilling the promise that in his early manhood he thought he had seen. As Henry Nash Smith wrote in 1958: "He had bet too much on the doctrine of Progress and the belief in an orderly benign universe to be able to emulate the younger writers who in his old age were finding literary capital in the master image of the Waste Land and were beginning to produce a whole literature of alienation."

The great humorists of other nations and ages have been pessimists also; witness Molière and Swift. There were pessimists among Mark Twain's predecessors and contemporaries. Harry Levin has emphasized "the power of blackness" in Poe, Hawthorne, and Melville, authors who could not share the optimistic attitude of Emerson and Whitman. There were pessimists among Mark Twain's contemporaries, notably Henry Adams, Ambrose Bierce, Thomas Hardy, Samuel Butler, and the aging Carlyle. There is a strain of pessimism in Edward Fitzgerald's *The Rubáiyát of Omar Khayyám* and in James Thomson's *The City of Dreadful Night*. Meanwhile in the United States writers who are not to be classed as pessimists—Lowell, Howells, and Whitman—had lost much of their faith in the innate goodness of human nature and now saw that the republic was not fulfilling the promise of its earlier years.

Since his death in 1910 critics of every variety have had their say about Mark Twain's life and writings: impressionists, formalists, symbolists, New Humanists, Marxists, Freudians, and various others. They have pointed to artistic defects in even the greatest of his books, and they have noted that the great bulk of his published work has little intrinsic importance; and yet for most of them he is still one of our greatest writers. For the literary critic Mark Twain poses two special problems. First, he was a great humorist, and Brooks and other critics with little taste for humor have had great difficulty in assessing the value of his books. In the second place, Mark Twain was and still is enormously popular, and this disturbs the modern critics who seem to value only those writers whom they regard as alienated from society. This, it seems to me, is a main reason why they have made so much of his pessimism.

Mark Twain's influence has been greatest on writers of fiction, and it is greater than that of any other American writer except Henry James. Hemingway doubtless spoke for others besides himself, notably Faulkner, when in 1935 he wrote in *The Green Hills of Africa:*

> All modern American literature comes from one book by Mark Twain called *Huckleberry Finn*. If you read it you must stop where the Nigger Jim is stolen from the boys. That is the real end. The rest is just cheating. But it's the best book we've had. All American writing comes from that. There was nothing before. There has been nothing as good since.

Tony Tanner

The Pond of Youth

> *But our wiser years still run back to the despised recollections of childhood, and always we are fishing up some wonderful article out of that pond.*—Emerson, *Essays,* "Intellect"

> *Jean's spirits are good; Clara's are rising. They have youth—the only thing that was worth giving to the race.*—Clemens in a letter to Howells after the death of his daughter Susy

The older Clemens became the more obsessed with youth he was: indeed his first important works show a chronologically regressive curve. Mark Twain in Europe is followed by Mark Twain in the West who in turn is followed by Mark Twain as a cub-pilot on the Mississippi: the reverse order to the actual sequence of Clemens's own life. By the time of *Huckleberry Finn* he has chosen to write as a child. . . . There were stylistic and moral reasons for this chosen point of view, but the strategy of the child-narrator would not have occurred to Clemens had he not felt an increasing tug backwards into the past, his own and America's. And from it he fished up his most wonderful articles. The sense of release, the unhindered flow of his autobiography when he returns to his childhood, gives evidence of a very special sort of "feel" for the past which cannot be explained by normal wistfulness.

From The Reign of Wonder: Naivety and Reality in American Literature, *by Tony Tanner. Cambridge: Cambridge University Press, 1965. Copyright © by Cambridge University Press.*

As I have said, I spent some part of every year at the farm until I was twelve or thirteen years old. The life which I led there with my cousins was full of charm, and so is the memory of it yet. I can call back the solemn twilight and mystery of the deep woods, the earthy smells, the faint odors of the wild flowers, the sheen of rain-washed foliage, the rattling clatter of drops when the wind shook the trees, the far-off hammering of woodpeckers and the muffled drumming of wood pheasants in the remoteness of the forest, the snapshot glimpses of disturbed wild creatures scurrying through the grass—I can call it all back and make it as real as it ever was, and as blessed.[1]

This particular passage continues for some pages, effortless and unflagging in its detailed sensory recreation of the minutiae of his life as a child. "The first step" was the most vivid for Clemens, and no subsequent experience obliterated or blurred his early sense impressions which up to his death he could recount with a matchless relaxed verve. And indeed shortly before his death he showed his preference for youth by forming an imaginary organization called the Aquarium which was composed of young schoolgirls with whom he talked and corresponded. As he grew older, references to "the old times when we laughed"[2] and "the reviving wine of the past, the pathetic past, the beautiful past, the dear and lamented past"[3] proliferated in his letters and notebooks. He came to regard the following snatch of poetry

> The day when we went gipsying
> A long time ago

as one of the "two most pathetic, moving things in the English tongue,"[4] and Henry Nash Smith is surely right to say that the line had "powerful incantatory and talismanic values"[5] for Clemens. His second "most pathetic moving thing" was simply the phrase "Departed this life,"[6] and it reveals the inevitable hatred of old age and death which is inextricably associated with the idealization of youth. As he

[1]*The Autobiography of Mark Twain,* ed. Charles Neider (New York: Harper and Bros., 1959) pp. 12–13.

[2]*Works,* vol. xxxv, (New York: Gabriel Wells, 1923–25) p. 773.

[3]*Autobiography,* p. 40.

[4]*Mark Twain's Notebook,* ed. Albert B. Paine, (New York: Harper and Bros., 1935) p. 319; also Notebook 31 (II), 13 Dec. 1896–6 Jan., 1897, MTP [Mark Twain Papers, University of California, Berkeley] TS, p. 50. Copyright © 1963 by the Mark Twain Company.

[5]*Mark Twain-Howells Letters,* vol. II, ed. Henry Nash Smith and William M. Gibson (Cambridge, Mass.: Harvard University Press), p. 686 (see footnote).

[6]*Mark Twain's Notebook,* ed. Paine, p. 319.

reminisces about his boyhood friends in his autobiography, he finds himself writing the same sad refrain over and over again. *"He died. It is what I have to say about so many of those boys and girls."*[7] When he recounts meetings with old friends in later life, he reveals how he always looked for evidence of the ghost of youth imprisoned in the aging body. "I saw Tom Nash approaching me across a vacant space and I walked toward him, for I recognized him at once. He was old and white-headed, but the boy of fifteen was still visible in him."[8] . . . "the boy to whom I had told the cat story when we were callow juveniles was still present in that cheerful little old man."[9] Age is only ever a terrible decline, a cruel and inexplicable process of deprivation. "It is a pity that we cannot escape from life when we are young,"[10] he wrote with complete sincerity. And when his beloved daughter Susy died, he stated the sentiment even more revealingly: "Susy died at the right time, the fortunate time of life, the happy age—twenty four years. At twenty four such a girl has seen the best of life—life as a happy dream. After that age the risks begin: responsibility comes, and with it the cares, the sorrows, and the inevitable tragedy."[11] Clemens could only envisage youth and age as existing in a state of almost grotesque oppugnancy. For instance, in his notebooks he records a plan to write a sketch in which two sets of people—one young, one old—visit a house which is transformed into a fairy palace during the night. They are subjected to a sort of vice-versa in which they keep their respective faces and for the rest acquire opposite characteristics. The young faces have old bodies and are full of incomprehensible sorrow; the old faces are joined to delightedly young bodies and only vaguely remember a sort of nightmare in which they were once old people. The spell is dissolved in the morning, leaving the proper young to match up with each other, and the old begging the chief fairy to restore their lost youth. Being refused they march off to a solemn chant.[12] Age appears as a terrible remorseless sentence: a punishment, a blight, an end of joy which is visited on the human race for no apparent reason. This is surely something different from the usual syndrome of emotions which attend upon old age. By way of compensation it was this loathing for old age which seems to have given Clemens's writing about youth its fantastic vividness. When he saw the world innocently, when he viewed it

[7]*Autobiography*, p. 71.
[8]*Ibid*. p. 37.
[9]*Ibid*. p. 74.
[10]*Ibid*. p. 126.
[11]*Works*, vol. xxxvii, p. 146.
[12]Notebook 31 (II), 13 Dec. 1896–6 Jan. 1897, MTP TS, pp. 41–3. Copyright © 1963 by the Mark Twain Company.

naively, when the senses were discovering the color and texture of reality as for the first time—when he responded to things as Huck does; then that was life, the best the world had to offer.

Clemens's preoccupation with "youth" would require a book in itself to probe properly, but we can suggest the important relationship between Clemens the man and Huck, his youthful creation, by noting his response to one of Howells's novels. Two years after Clemens had finished *Huckleberry Finn,* Howells published *Indian Summer.* This is the story of Theodore Colville who, at forty-one, is depressed by the onset of middle-age and seeks temporarily to regain his youth by attaching himself to the youthful, beautiful Imogene Graham. The theme is very simply developed. When Colville watches Imogene at a dance we read: "Her *abandon* interested Colville, and then awed him; the spectacle of that young unjaded capacity for pleasure touched him with a profound sense of loss."[13] When out walking with Imogene in Florence he asks about the Cascine:

> "Do they keep the fountain of youth turned on here during the winter still?"
> "I've never seen it," said Imogene gaily.
> "Of course not. You never looked for it. Neither did I when I was here before. But it wouldn't escape me now."[14]

Occasionally Howells gives up flirting with symbolism (he makes some heavy points out of the contrast between Spring and Winter) and states his theme outright:

> "Perhaps you'll find out after a while that I'm not an old fellow either, but only a 'Lost Youth'."[15]

After a few remarks in this vein Imogene decides that it is her mission to restore his youth:

> "I want you to feel that *I* am your youth—the youth you were robbed of—given back to you."[16]

It becomes increasingly obvious that he is *not* young, that they are hopelessly unsuited: a convenient accident with a bolting horse puts

[13]William Dean Howells, *Indian Summer* (Boston: Ticknor, 1886), p. 75.
[14]*Ibid.* p. 92.
[15]*Ibid.* p. 149.
[16]*Ibid.* p. 277.

Colville out of his senses but restores Imogene to hers. She suddenly realizes that she has no love for him and in one of those tired happy endings which Howells borrowed from the sentimental tradition, Colville marries Mrs. Bower who, being in the flower of middle-age, is ideal for him. In a conversation between them Howells reiterates his theme. They have just heard some singing in the street.

> "I heard just such singing before I fell asleep the night after the party at Madame Uccelli's, and it filled me with fury."
> "Why should it do that?"
> "I don't know. It seemed like voices from our youth—Lina."
> She had no resentment of his use of her name in the tone with which she asked: "Did you hate that so much?"
> "No; the loss of it."
> They both fetched a deep breath.[17]

The mere mention of Youth seems to have made an extraordinary number of Howells's contemporaries fetch a deep breath. Excursions into childhood were common—Howells's own *Boy's Town* and Aldrich's *Story of a Bad Boy* are two examples—and quite far apart from the normal regrets associated with growing old there is a special cultural factor involved: namely the fact that people who, like Clemens and Howells, were middle-aged in the 1880's had spent their childhood in the Eden of pre-Civil-War America. Dismay with the harsh reality of post-war corruption and the spoliation of the continent thrust them back to the psychic reality of their youth. That they were acutely aware of the break the war caused is hinted at in Howells's novel. During his first conversation with Imogene, Colville mentions an old song which she doesn't recognize.

> "Ah, I see," said Colville, peering at her under his thoughtfully knitted brows, "you do belong to another era. You don't remember the old negro minstrel song."
> "No," said Miss Graham. "I can only remember the end of the war."
> "How divinely young!" said Colville.[18]

We might recall that it was Howells who gave James the seed of his novel *The Ambassadors* which emerged in Strether's important speech to little Bilham: "All the same, don't forget that you're

[17]*Ibid.* pp. 371–372.
[18]*Ibid.* p. 44.

young—blessedly young; be glad of it, on the contrary, and live up to it. Live all you can—it's a mistake not to.''[19] And James himself very succinctly describes the difference that the Civil War made to those Americans who knew both the previous and subsequent Americas:

> The subsidence of that great convulsion had left a different tone from the tone it found, and one may say that the Civil War marks an era in the history of the American mind. It introduced into the national consciousness a certain sense of proportion and relation, of the world being a more complicated place than it had hitherto seemed, the future more treacherous, success more difficult . . . the good American, in days to come, will be a more critical person than his complacent and confident grandfather. He has eaten of the tree of knowledge.[20]

The Civil War was a fall—*the* fall for those who experienced it, and consequently, youth, for those who had spent it before the war, took on a paradisiacal, mythical glow. Conversely to grow old in postwar America—an America "rotten, as far as the dollar is concerned''[21] in Clemens's own words—was to experience age as a doubly ugly thing. Bearing all this in mind, consider Clemens's reaction when he had read *Indian Summer*. He wrote immediately and heartfeltly to Howells:

> It is a beautiful story, & makes a body laugh all the time, & cry inside, & feel so old & so forlorn; & gives him gracious glimpses of his lost youth that fill him with a measureless regret, & build up in him a cloudy sense of his having been a prince, once, in some enchanted far off land, & of being in exile now, & desolate—& lord, no chance ever to get back there again! That is the thing that hurts.[22]

What is interesting is not only the general sentiment of the piece but the tone—which is in fact very different from the rest of the letter: it is different for this very simple reason, that Clemens has started to talk like Huck Finn. He would not have let Huck say "measureless regret" or "cloudy sense" perhaps, but the syntax, the air of spontaneity, the feeling of almost breathless sincerity—these are Huck's. It is a classic example of how the mere mention of youth could bring out the Huck Finn in Clemens, as though only through that lad could Clemens articulate his most important feelings. Small wonder that his wife nicknamed him "Youth." According to Jung, in times of stress, deprivation or

[19]Henry James, *The Ambassadors*, vol. I (London: Macmillan, 1923), p. 190.
[20]Henry James, *Hawthorne* (Ithaca, N.Y.: Cornell University Press, 1956), p. 114.
[21]*Autobiography*, p. 121.
[22]*Mark Twain-Howells Letters*, pp. 534–5.

frustration, it is possible for a person unconsciously to reactivate earlier forms of adaptation to life, and without wishing to attempt any superficial psychoanalysis of Clemens it can fairly be said that the more he felt old age and post-war America to constitute a double state of exile, the happier he felt when he could recover, if only through writing, his innocent youthful intimacy with a lost past.

An important extension of Clemens's preoccupation with youth was his lifelong interest in youthful modes of thought and expression. And it is important to remember that what gives Huck Finn's speech much of its lyric and moral force is not simply that he speaks in the vernacular but that he also speaks and thinks as a child. It would be a mistake to suggest that Clemens found a nourishing precedent for his own work in the writing of children, but if we say in general that, as a writer, he was after a habitual economy of sincere simplicity to oppose to the inflated rhetoric and attitudinizing endorsed by the official culture; then we may also say that a childish artlessness could be as much to his purpose as vernacular irreverence. And as early as 1864 while he was still a reporter for the *Territorial Enterprise* we find evidence of an interest in childish modes of expression. In one of his letters to that paper he gives a humorous account of a visit to the local school during which the children read their compositions:

> The "compositions" read to-day were as exactly like the compositions I used to hear read in our school as one baby's nose is exactly like all other babies' noses. I mean the old principal ear-marks were all there: the cutting to the bone of the subject with the very first gash, without any preliminary foolishness in the way of a gorgeous introductory: the inevitable and persevering tautology; the brief, monosyllabic sentences (beginning as a very general thing, with the pronoun "I"); the penchant for presenting rigid, uncompromising facts for the consideration of the hearer, rather than ornamental fancies; the depending for success of the composition upon its general merits, without tacking artificial aides to the end of it, in the shape of deductions or conclusions, or clap-trap climaxes, albeit their absence sometimes imparts to these essays the semblance of having come to an end before they were finished—of arriving at full speed at a jumping-off place and going suddenly overboard, as it were, leaving a sensation such as one feels when he stumbles without warning upon that infernal "To be Continued" in the midst of a thrilling magazine story. I know there are other styles of school composition, but these are the characteristics of the style which I have in my eye at present. I do not know why this one has particularly suggested itself to my mind, unless the literary effort of one of the boys there to-day left me with an unusually vivid impression. It ran something in this wise:

COMPOSITION

"I like horses. Where we lived before we came here, we used to have a cutter and horses. We used to ride in it. I like Winter. I like snow. I used to have a pony all to myself, where I used to live before I came here. Once it drifted a good deal—very deep—and when it stopped I went out and got in it."

That was all. There was no climax to it, except the spasmodic bow which the tautological little student jerked at the school as he closed his labours.[23]

Along with this piece I want to consider an extract from an essay called "A Complaint about Correspondents" which he wrote soon after. He is complaining about the mannerisms of letter writers in the East and goes on to say:

The most useful and interesting letters we get here from home are from children seven or eight years old. This is petrified truth. Happily they have got nothing to talk about but home, and neighbors, and family—things their betters think unworthy of transmission thousands of miles. They write simply and naturally, and without straining for effect. They tell all they know, and then stop. They seldom deal in abstractions or moral homilies. Consequently their epistles are brief; but, treating as they do of familiar scenes and persons, always entertaining. Now, therefore, if you would learn the art of letter-writing, let a child teach you.[24]

And after quoting from a letter from a child which is extremely naive and marked by a random honesty, he comments: "This child treads on my toes, in every other sentence, with a perfect looseness, but in the simplicity of her time of life she doesn't know it."[25] One might immediately point out that in the simplicity of his time of life Huck was to tread on the moral toes of a civilization, and it was his very unconsciousness of doing so that gave it such force. But more interesting are the virtues which Clemens, thus early, ascribes to children's writing. "Rigid uncompromising facts . . . rather than ornamental fancies", "cutting to the bone of the subject with the very first gash," the abrupt endings which flaunt the tradition of contrived climax, the absence of straining for effect, the reverence of familiar details, the suspicion of

[23]Henry Nash Smith and Frederick Anderson, eds., *Mark Twain of the Enterprise* (Berkeley: University of California Press, 1957), pp. 136–7.

[24]Mark Twain, *The Celebrated Jumping Frog of Calaveras County and other sketches* (New York: Webb, 1867), p. 31.

[25]Ibid. pp. 32–3.

abstractions, the avoidance of moral uplift—these, I submit, are all qualities which Clemens himself sought for, and which many subsequent American writers have incorporated into their writing. With little modification comparable terms occur in any discussion of writers like Hemingway (who himself said, "It is years since I added the wow to the end of a story"), Anderson, Stein, McCullers. Direct influence is, of course, not being argued, but that a cultivated naivety of speech and vision is evident in Clemens and such later writers seems to me irrefutable. What Clemens, half smilingly, noticed children doing unconsciously, he found analogous to his own ideals as writer. The evidence that this was so is recurrent. Here, for instance, is an extract from a letter he wrote to a young boy named Wattie Bowser while he was engaged in writing *Huckleberry Finn*. Bowser had sent him a composition on why he would like to be Mark Twain: the great man answered at length and included this praise:

> I have read your composition, and I think it is a very creditable performance. I notice that you use plain, simple language, short words, and brief sentences. That is the way to write English—it is the modern way, and the best way. Stick to it; don't let fluff and flowers and verbosity creep in. When you catch an adjective, kill it. No, I don't mean that utterly, but kill the most of them then the rest will be valuable. They weaken when they are close together, they give strength when they are far apart. An adjective-habit, or a wordy, diffuse, or flowery habit once fastened upon a person, is as hard to get rid of as any other vice.[26]

Much that is bad in nineteenth-century romantic writing—English and American—can be put down to the plague of unemployed epithets which settled on literature and robbed it of much of its ability to pay any clear-eyed, simple, trenchant attention to the empirical facts of the world. The simple sense units of children's writing, so ignorant of current literary conventions, so refreshingly off-hand and to the point, clearly occurred to Clemens as one way of avoiding the worst vices of the grand manner. Both the anti-social speech of the outlaw and the pre-social speech of the child suggested modes of escape to him. Just as he once planned to introduce a vernacular rebel into *Hamlet* to mock Shakespeare,[27] so he also suggested to Howells an article based on "A

[26]Letter to Wattie Bowser, March 20, 1880. First published in *Houston Post*, Sunday, Feb. 7, 1960.
[27]*Mark Twain-Howells Letters*, p. 369.

38   *Tony Tanner*

Boy's Comments Upon Homer".[28] In both cases the revered literary object was to be deflated by a low, a naive, non-literary point of view. Two other instances of his interest in children's writing are worth quoting in order to substantiate the claim that Clemens evinced a life-long interest in it which was more than just humorous. In 1887 a school teacher, Miss Caroline B. LeRow, sent Clemens a collection of amusing linguistic errors by her pupils which she had collected during her teaching, asking him if she should publish them. He said she should and also wrote a review of the book in *The Century* called "English as She is Taught". For Clemens, the mistakes that the children made prove two things. First, that education is conducted in a most unenlightened way: "All through this little book one detects the signs of a certain probable fact—that a large part of the pupil's 'instruction' consists in cramming him with obscure and wordy 'rules' which he does not understand and has not time to understand".[29] He calls the culture which produces such a method of education "a brickbat culture".[30] Secondly, he maintained that the mistakes demonstrated the spontaneous simplicity of a child's mind, and its essential inaptness for rigid, coercive rules. As we have seen, he himself worked to perfect a loose, permissive, flexible, formless way of writing and to see children trained out of these virtues which they enjoyed by instinct annoyed him. One of the mistakes quoted in the book pleased him so much that he sent it to Howells repeating the comment he made in his review: "It is full of naïveté, brutal truth, and unembarrassed directness, and is the funniest (genuine) boy's composition I think I have ever seen".[31] His interest may be merely comic here, but "naïveté, brutal truth, and unembarrassed directness" are not bad terms for stressing some of the qualities of Huck's own speech.

Finally, it would not do to forget Clemens's delight in his daughter Susy's biography of himself. He quotes from it continually throughout his autobiography. Of course there is the normal parental attachment to the engagingly naive production of his adored child, but his comment on her way of writing has a broader significance. Thus in his autobiography:

> I cannot bring myself to change any line or word in Susy's sketch of me, but will introduce passages from it now and then just as they come in —their quaint simplicity out of her honest heart, which was the beautiful heart of a child. What comes from that source has a charm and grace of its

[28]*Ibid*. vol. 1, p. 105.
[29]*Works,* vol. xxvi, p. 254.
[30]*Ibid*.
[31]*Ibid*.

own which may transgress all the recognized laws of literature, if it
choose, and yet be literature still, and worthy of hospitality.[32]

He also refuses to correct her spelling on the by-now recognizable
grounds that "it would take from it its freedom and flexibility and make
it stiff and formal."[33] Clemens seems to have been one of the first
American writers to feel that the whole prescribed cultural orthodoxy of
the official genteel culture was altogether too "stiff and formal" and
that what was needed was more "freedom and flexibility," something
more simple and natural—something, in a sense, more child-like. And
many of his scattered critical judgments echo his terms of praise for
children's writing that we have so far examined. For instance, he
praises a minor writer called Sage on the grounds of "an artlessness, an
absence of self-consciousness, ditto of striving after effect"[34] and he
admired Howe's *Story of a Country Town* because it was "so simple,
sincere, direct and at the same time so clear and strong."[35] On similar
grounds he vigorously defended General Grant's style against the rather
precious and pedantic criticisms of Matthew Arnold.

What most significantly emerges from all these comments on
children's writing is an undertow of primitivism—"the beautiful heart
of the child" always expresses itself well no matter how formlessly,
until it is circumscribed and crippled by social and literary rules. In
abandoning high rhetoric for the low vernacular, in supplanting the
social conformist by the anti-social outlaw, in moving back from age to
youth and preferring untutored naivety to formally educated maturity,
Clemens effected a triple rebellion of major importance for American
literature: and it is worth noting that in every case the rebellion involves
a renunciation of established society and the accepted achievements of
civilization. The young vernacular rebel is alone with his wonder, his
candor, his sound heart.

[32]*Autobiography,* p. 202.
[33]*Ibid.*
[34]*Mark Twain-Howells Letters,* vol. 1, p. 138.
[35]*Ibid.* vol. II, p. 492.

Howard Mumford Jones

The Pessimism of Mark Twain

I

Bernard DeVoto somewhere remarks that you can quote Mark Twain on almost any side of any question, and the student soon discovers this is true. Thus Twain wrote an essay excoriating King Leopold's cruelty in the Congo and another one denouncing Western imperialism; yet, after going around the world, when he published *Following the Equator,* he was full of praise for the British empire because it had imposed cleanliness, order, and a sense for progress upon the countries the British occupied. In a book on Christian Science he denounced Mrs. Eddy as essentially fraudulent as a prophet and essentially crafty as a businesswoman; but he told his official biographer, Albert Bigelow Paine, that Mrs. Eddy likely deserved a place in the Trinity as much as the other members of it because she had organized a healing principle that had been employed for two thousand years as mere guesswork. No one was more vituperative than he about the covetousness of the robber barons, and the novel by Twain and Warner, *The Gilded Age,* gave its name to that period. Twain, however, sought to make money by seeking out and owning monopolies as they did, he had golden visions of easy wealth, and in his lawless egotism he resembled the millionaires whom he denounced. He had no use for kings, so that *A Connecticut Yankee in King Arthur's Court* was written among other purposes to ridicule monarchy; but Twain gloried in the attention paid him by William II of Germany, the Prince of Wales, and the Austrian royal family. Indeed, his essay on the assassination of the Austrian empress soon

From Belief and Disbelief in American Literature, *by Howard Mumford Jones (Chicago and London: The University of Chicago Press, 1969). Reprinted by permission of the Frank L. Weil Institute. Copyright © 1967, Frank L. Weil Institute.*

leaves this theme for a dazzle of rhetorical delight in the pomp of a military funeral illustrating the might of imperial power. Twain delighted to ridicule bathos; he thought, however, that his sentimental *The Prince and the Pauper* was a better work of art than *The Adventures of Tom Sawyer,* and regarded the equally sentimental *Personal Recollections of Joan of Arc* as his literary masterpiece. These conflicts were, apparently, built into him. The genial humorist of William Dean Howells's *My Mark Twain,* printed in 1910, is one side of him, and the tortured personality of Justin Kaplan's magisterial *Mr. Clemens and Mark Twain,* published in 1966, is another.

Such complexities have to be sorted out, and there is an inevitable tendency to arrange the components of Twain's personality in pairs, or, as Emerson would say, polarities. During most of the humorist's life the polarities were between the picture of Twain as a popular funny man, and the emerging assumption that he was a literary genius. Another set of contradictory interpretations is represented by two notable early studies: Van Wyck Brooks's *The Ordeal of Mark Twain,* which argued in 1920 that a naive Western genius was made to submit to the genteel tradition as represented by Mrs. Clemens and Twain's literary friend, Howells; and DeVoto's *Mark Twain's America,* which maintained in 1932 that Brooks knew nothing about either Missouri or the West and that Twain was from the beginning a conscious Western literary artist. I suppose a third rearrangement is implicit in the subtitle of DeLancey Ferguson's excellent biography of 1943, *Mark Twain: Man and Legend.* By the forties the public personality of Clemens had developed into legend, but there was now far more material at hand to use for painting the actual man.

When one asks what Twain really believed about God, man, and the universe, is there any way to fuse these opposites into a single pair? I think there is. The contradictions that make Twain interesting from this point of view seem to me to arise from the fact that from an early period there was in him an acceptance, perhaps naïve, of eighteenth-century rationalism, which easily absorbed into itself doctrines of comparative religion and of evolution dominant in the nineteenth century. But there was also from boyhood an opposite tendency, a kind of romantic sensibility which looks like nineteenth-century subjectivism and in one sense is that, but which really descends from eighteenth-century sentimentalism in both the popular and the philosophic sense. In Twain the spirits of Voltaire and Rousseau fought for control. In him the deism of Tom Paine and the materialism of somebody like Haeckel struggled with a stubborn temperamental conviction that individual goodness counts—a belief all his naïve determinism could never extinguish.

Twain denounced all organized religion, and, in his privately printed "gospel" of 1906, *What Is Man?* he stripped the human being of free will and destroyed the possibility of self-determined personal development. Yet Twain's best friend, aside from Howells, was the Rev. Joseph Twichell of Hartford; and Twain always had a weakness for clergymen unless, like the Rev. Mr. Sabine, who refused to bury an actor from his New York church, they seemed to him sanctimonious. He told Paine in 1903, "Who can doubt that society in heaven consists of mainly undesirable persons?" But when Twain's wife died in 1904, he had this inscription engraved on her tombstone: "Gott sei dir gnädig, O meine Wonne!" It is difficult to see how God could be gracious to Olivia Clemens in the afterlife unless there was some heaven for her to go to. Yet Twain had earlier declared that if God had prepared such a place for us and really wanted us to know about it, He could have found some better medium of communication than the Bible, a book "so liable to alterations and misinterpretation." The point is not to trap the great humorist—it is absurdly easy to do so; the point is to try to comprehend the major phases of his erratic development in the matter of belief.

II

It is commonly held that the determinism of *What Is Man?* and the general pessimism of Twain's utterance about the human race are products of the Calvinism that was drilled into him in boyhood. Calvinism is, however, an intricate system of ideas that has many variants, and I think those who really accepted Calvinism and later broke with it all had to go through a period of spiritual agony. I do not find any such period in Twain's biography—anything resembling that chronicled in, for example, William Hale White's *The Autobiography of Mark Rutherford,* which is only partly fiction, or in Edmund Gosse's *Father and Son,* which is wholly fact. The simple village preaching and the simple village teaching to which young Samuel Clemens was exposed contained nothing, so far as I can see, like "Sinners in the Hands of an Angry God," however revivalism may have described damnation. Religion in Hannibal seems to have been the standard religion of the Bible belt. It is true that in both *Tom Sawyer* and *Huck Finn* Twain plays up the boys' fear of damnation, fear of the devil, and fear of instant judgment if they do something wrong. He also plays up their fear of witchcraft. Are we therefore to argue that witchcraft was generally taught in the churches? Most of our information about Sam Clemens's boyhood and his boyhood religion comes from Sam Clemens, the adult writer, so that it is difficult to know how much is true and how much is imagined in his recollections. Young Sam detested Sunday school and church-going as most boys do; like any other boy he was afraid of God and juvenile about the meaning of prayer. He also picked up a good deal of folklore from the Negroes and from his playmates. But I am unable to see much dour Calvinism in this experience. If he had been taught any kind of Calvinism, and if this had been really ground into him, we should have heard later how he struggled with the concepts of damnation, election, and efficacious grace through Jesus Christ, but, except for the chapters on Palestine in *Innocents Abroad,* where Twain could not avoid the topic, the name of Jesus scarcely appears in his work. He concentrates on God—on the concept of a Christian God, which Twain thinks of as a human invention designed to flatter mankind into the belief that man is of any consequence in the universe.

From 1853, when he left home, until 1870, when he married Olivia Langdon, Samuel Clemens was a wanderer on the face of the earth—a wandering printer, a wandering newspaperman, a wandering writer, a Mississippi River pilot traveling up and down some 1400 miles of shifting channel, an amateur miner, a popular lecturer of the comic kind, and on occasions virtually a vagabond. Much of this period was spent on the frontier; for instance, Nevada, or in territory that had recently been frontier territory; for example, the great river. There were cities, towns, hamlets, and plantations along the Mississippi exhibiting considerable culture, but the restless population of the stream itself was made up of raftsmen, keelboatmen, gamblers, fancy women, slave-traders with their coffles of human merchandise, roustabouts, profane mates, itinerant evangelists, medicine men, and other like human types, most of them rakish, few of them having any permanent place in stable society. A journeyman printer, moreover, sees more of the seamy side of life than he does of its gentler aspects. A newspaperman is usually better acquainted with sinfulness than he is with salvation. Nevada, when Twain went there, was a boom-and-bust frontier area, and so were the parts of California he knew. The Hawaiian Islands were less crude, but at this time they were in a state I can describe only as a quiet and comfortable anarchy.

As a lecturer after 1866 Twain knew more about hotels than he did about homes; and when he joined the *Quaker City* excursion to the Mediterranean in 1867, he was still the rover, still the wild humorist of the Pacific slope, still the restless younger man conscious of talent but ignorant of the proper channel through which to direct its flow. Twain did not achieve anything resembling stability until he was about forty.

For twenty years his experience had been of the capriciousness of luck, the meaninglessness of mere good will, the crass cruelty of chance, as when the steamboat *Pennsylvania* blew up and killed 150 persons, including his brother, the amiable Henry Clemens. The God who seemed to preside over the anarchy that ruled the world from the Mississippi to the Hawaiian Islands was no genteel Christian deity, but the indifferent God of Thomas Hardy. Twain's twenty years of wandering were, I suggest, far more influential in molding his outlook than the mild Christianity of Hannibal, Missouri, which in later years seemed to him an utterly inadequate explanation of the ways of God to man.

I believe one can distinguish three shaping elements in these decades. The first is that during these years, Clemens read enormously at every opportunity and that much of his reading had an eighteenth-century basis or bias, whether it was *Songs in Many Keys* by that most Augustan of Boston poets, Oliver Wendell Holmes, virtually memorized by Twain when he was ill in Hawaii, or the three great memoir writers whom he read and reread—Saint-Simon, Pepys, and Casanova. He seems to have used Voltaire as a means for learning French. Above all, while he was a pilot, he saturated himself in Paine's *The Age of Reason,* so that when, on the *Quaker City* excursion, he read the Bible with some care as a guide to Palestine, he approached religious doctrine with a deistic bias. One should add that he was fascinated by science, particularly astronomy and geology, and could conceive of no other universe than the Newtonian one.

A second episode of basic importance was Twain's meeting with an enigmatic Scotsman named MacFarlane in Cincinnati in 1856-57. It is possible that MacFarlane never existed. If he did, he lived by himself, he was a serious-minded worker, and he had read widely in contemporary science and philosophy. He believed in evolution, regarding man as a failure, the only animal capable of malice and uncleanliness. If Twain is to be trusted, MacFarlane apparently laid the foundation for the humorist's future conviction that the moral sense in man is what degrades him below the animals

The third impact of these years, particularly those on the Mississippi and covering his experiences in the Far West, was brooding over vastness—the vastness of nights on the river when, alone in the pilot-house, he had to travel through darkness, the vastness of the starry heavens, the immense indifference of sky and land in the Nevada desert and of sky and sea in the Pacific, where most of the crew of the *Hornet* had miserably perished. He adopted the Newtonian view that the universe is an immense machine created and supervised by an infinitely remote engineer. He adopted also from his readings in popular astronomy concepts of the enormity of space and the littleness of the solar system. Seeing then and later the perpetual imbecility of the human race, having small opportunity and no desire to attend church services, he arrived early at the conclusion that Christian altruism, Christian salvation, Christian benevolence were incompetent measures of the majestic indifference of God, the mercilessness of the heavens, and the unbreakable chain that bound one event to its successor. These views he long suppressed or put aside, though they lurk in much that he wrote from *Innocents Abroad* to *Pudd'nhead Wilson,* and though they appear, imaginatively powerful or logically expressed, in such works as *The Man That Corrupted Hadleyburg, The $30,000 Bequest,* and *Was It Heaven or Hell?* and, more powerfully still, in posthumous works like *The Mysterious Stranger* and *Letters from the Earth.* Of course there is also *What Is Man?,* a book that gets its title from the Psalms: "What is man, that thou regardest him, or the son of man, that thou visitest him?" Twain's answer is: "Not much."

Remembering that Mark Twain perpetually contradicts himself, I think we can yet sketch out the lines of his mature interpretation of God, man, and the universe. God is a being of majestical and unpredictable power, who in Twain's fiction retains most of the characteristics of the Christian deity as a *dramatis persona* except benevolence toward man, but whose essence Twain never clearly defines. God is, however, the ground of being of the universe, which, at some remote point in time He created by arbitrary fiat—or perhaps the fiat was not arbitrary, a point to which I shall come in a moment. What Twain means by the universe is not always clear. Mostly it is a universe of matter that works, or is worked upon, by mechanical principles. Yet, as Young Satan informs the boys in *The Mysterious Stranger,* the universe is a dream, they are dreams and God Himself is a dream. The point would be unimportant except that, after the manner of Newton and his commentators, Twain makes his deity give matter an initial push, a first action, and from this first act every other event mercilessly follows. Whether the law of cause and effect existed intellectually prior to the universe, so that the operation of matter had to conform to that law, Twain does not say, nor does he define deity in any clear and consistent terms. Does God conform to necessity, or is necessity something imposed upon the universe by God? In the splendid rhetorical opening of *Letters from the Earth* Mark Twain pictures creation after the manner of Milton and has the archangels comment on it, as do the archangels in Goethe's *Faust.* The attributes of Twain's deity, like his acts, are phrased in Christian terms, but his God is not a Christian God.

Although Mark Twain insists in *What Is Man?* and elsewhere—for example, in *Pudd'nhead Wilson*—upon mechanical necessity, the mechanical universe is somehow also an evolutionary universe, somewhat to the confusion of Twain's metaphor about man as a machine—a metaphor that carries one back to La Mettrie and other eighteenth-century French *philosophes*. As a machine, man has no control over his acts or his motives for action. He is merely an impersonal engine, moved, directed, and commanded, says Twain, by external influences only. He cannot think an original thought nor perform a uniquely self-willed action. Behind the elaborate façade of religious and ethical systems there is, says Twain, the basic truth that the only motive for action is self-approval. How a machine arrives at self-approval Twain does not quite explain. Yet man the machine can also, apparently of its own volition, place itself in circumstances that will, as this writer says, "train it" in an upward or downward direction, morally and socially. How a machine determines what is subjectively upward or down, again, is not made plain, and Twain seems content with a virtually insoluble paradox: Man is an impersonal engine commanded by external influences only, but this impersonal engine is also subjectively conscious of the need of nourishing its own self-approval.

This self-approval—and here, I take it, is Twain's attempt to get out of the difficulty—seems to be a function of conscience, which Twain describes as "that mysterious autocrat, lodged in a man, which compels the man to content its desires." Twain is again fuzzy. If conscience is something like Schopenhauer's irrational will, it is not conscience but something unconscious and instinctual; and if conscience is, as Twain says it is, indifferent to "man's greed," indifference to good fails to throw any light upon the origin of "good" as a way by which to measure the consciousness of being conscious of good. At times conscience seems to be a synonym for the Moral Sense, Twain's favorite whipping boy; but the moral sense, or at least a sense for the higher good, undergoes an odd transformation when the Old Man in the dialog tells the Young Man; "Diligently train your ideals upward and still upward toward a summit where you will find your chief pleasure in conduct which, while contenting you, will be sure to confer benefits upon your neighbor." This is a queer parallel to Adam Smith's theory that although all men regard their own individual interests only, each is led as by an invisible hand to work for the good of the whole; and the difficulty is not met by saying that idealism is simply another form of self-regard; the difficulty is to explain how any concept of public good can possibly arise.

What Is Man? purports to be a systematic treatise, but its logical difficulties are so patent as to require little further discussion. Obviously

Twain changes the concept of a machine to suit his argument. A machine is in fact a mechanical object lacking all consciousness and unable to perform the function for which it was built unless suitable outside force is intelligently applied to set it in motion. For Twain to talk about a machine of steel as being more "civilized" than a machine of stone is a case of a transferred epithet that conceals a logical error. Machines are not civilized; they are produced by civilization. Machines have no consciousness; man does. A machine cannot either by volition or instinct reproduce its kind. This is possible only to organisms, which, though they may have statistically predictable potentialities, are more than, or at least other than, mere elementary matter. No machine can train itself even in Twain's sense of moving, physically or psychologically, into some sort of social and temporal area where "outside influences"—his phrase—will somehow improve the machine morally, intellectually, or socially. Machines can be improved mechanically but not otherwise. In truth Twain never distinguished between a mechanical concept like that of a machine and a biological concept like that of an organism.

His basic assumption is of course that of much modern science until the twentieth century: the iron necessity in cause and effect as the "explanation" of events. It was axiomatic and primary in most of the books about science that he read. If one wanted to take Twain's assumption seriously, one would have to point out that in our time Heisenberg's uncertainty principle damages this primary postulate beyond repair. The principles of the new physics, as Arthur H. Compton has said, cannot predict any event; they can tell only the chance of its occurrence. Even the behavior of an organism is not something that can be definitely determined; the utmost one can say is that its behavior will fall within certain principles or limits of probability. But statistics of chance are one thing; necessity is another. The curious thing is that Twain, despite his argument, was imaginatively enlisted on the side of chance. Thus in *The Mysterious Stranger* Young Satan, who possesses supernal power, at the request of the boys of Eseldorf actively interferes to change the already determined patterns of the lives of some of the villagers. How, if the iron law of necessity rules the universe, can even an archangel alter the course of events, especially in view of the fact that Twain says elsewhere, "Even the Almighty Himself cannot check or change [the] sequence of events once it is started"? Is an angel somehow more powerful than the Almighty?

III

It is of course possible, as DeVoto remarks, that the gospel of *What Is Man?* is not really a serious statement of determinism but rather a plea for pardon. If man is helpless, man cannot be blamed for anything. This is emotionally possible; yet the logical difficulty arises: who is to do the pardoning? And at this point some suspicion of a Calvinist influence truly arises, since, if God determines all, God is the only competent pardoning power. On the other hand, if the iron law of necessity existed anterior to the fiat of God, not even God is competent to forgive, unless, indeed, we blur all distinctions and declare that everything is as it is because it is as it is—a generalization that gets us precisely nowhere for it strips all words of all general meanings.

However this may be, we are dealing with a great imaginative writer, not with a metaphysician; and when we turn to Twain's concept of what he often referred to as the damned human race, we find a continuing tension between the ideas of Voltaire and the ideas of Rousseau; or, more particularly, we find that Twain in his maturer years takes over the notion of Swift, who said he hated and detested that animal called man, although he heartily loved John, Peter, Thomas, and so forth.

We may begin with some characteristic expressions of the darker view of man by Twain. The heir of all the ages in the foremost files of time seemed to our writer mostly a failure. He wrote somewhere that man was made at the end of the week's work when God was tired. He told Albert Bigelow Paine that man

> is a rickety sort of a thing, anyway you take him, a regular British Museum of infirmities and inferiorities. He is always undergoing repairs . . . man starts as a child and lives on diseases to the end as a regular diet . . . [Man is] the animal of the wig, the ear-trumpet, the glass eye, the porcelain teeth, the wooden leg, the trepanned skull, the silver windpipe—a creature that is mended and patched all over from top to bottom.

I quote only a part of this diatribe, which, however, ends by claiming for man one tremendous superiority over the other animals—in his imagination, his intellect. Yet on another occasion Twain informed Paine that anybody who knew anything knew that there was not a single life that was ever lived that was worth living.

The assumption that man's imagination marks his superiority appears many times in Twain, but this tribute is countered by the argument that in being gifted with a moral sense, man was given opportunity to degrade himself below the animals, and used it. This being true, only the mad can be happy. Satan in *The Mysterious Stranger* demonstrates to the boys that man's cruelty to man is always the product of the moral sense, but Twain's most straightforward statement about this degrading quality appears in a document posthumously published in *Letters from the Earth,* entitled "The Lowest Animal." Here are some statements from it:

> One is obliged to concede that in true loftiness of character, Man cannot claim to approach even the meanest of the Higher Animals. It is plain that he is constitutionally incapable of approaching that altitude; that he is constitutionally afflicted with a Defect which must make such approach forever impossible, for it is manifest that this defect is permanent in him, indestructible, ineradicable.
>
> I find this Defect to be the *Moral Sense.* He is the only animal that has it. It is the secret of degradation. It is the quality *which enables him to do wrong.* It has no other office. It is incapable of performing any other function. It could never have been intended to perform any other. Without it, man could do no wrong. He would rise at once to the level of the Higher Animals.
>
> It is as valueless to him as is disease. . . . What . . . do we find the Primal Curse to have been? Plainly what it was in the beginning: the infliction upon man of the Moral Sense; the ability to distinguish good from evil; and, with it, necessarily, the ability to *do* evil; for there can be no evil act without the presence of consciousness of it in the doer of it.[1]

The emotional tone of such passages is Swiftian, but the irony, though savage, has, as it were, a Voltairean base, since the concept of a moral sense or moral faculty was commonplace in eighteenth-century philosophy, and the reasoning behind Twain's satire is reasoning that derives its picture of man's imperfection by the use of Right Reason. I am of course using the term "eighteenth century" loosely and not chronologically.

Twain got himself into another logical difficulty. He holds, as we have seen, that man is a machine with no will of its own, that everything which happens is predetermined by an unbreakable chain of cause and effect beginning with some primordial act, that man is without free will, and that any progress which appears in humanity is solely the result of being somehow exposed to a better environment or conditioning. But this machine is also endowed with consciousness, and in *What Is Man?* Twain also gives it a conscience, although conscience is here not a function of free will but a mysterious autocrat lodged in man and com-

[1] Bernard DeVoto, ed., *Mark Twain, Letters from the Earth* (New York, 1962), pp. 228–229. The statement about man as a museum of infirmities is repeated in this essay.

pelling him to content its desires, which are apparently to be distinguished from the desires of the man who has the conscience. Conscience is likewise declared to be indifferent to the good of man, though what is meant by "good" does not clearly appear.

How does the moral sense fit into the machine? In all Twain's discussions of the moral sense he seems to assume that the moral sense enables man to know the good, yet, knowing the good, man invariably chooses evil. This choice must therefore be voluntary. We must then also assume either that the moral sense is part of the automatic functioning of man the machine, in which case praise and blame like good and evil are totally irrelevant; or that the moral sense, whether thought of as a faculty of the mind other than conscience or as some phase or function of consciousness, freely chooses to make value judgments, which man's willfulness invariably ignores and, in fact, uses as guides to proceed in the direction of evil rather than of good. I say that the moral sense must be a faculty of the mind other than conscience simply because Twain has elsewhere defined conscience as an autocrat which is other than free will and does not seek the good of man.

Whatever the confusion of Twain's logic, man is for him, patently, a hypocritical being. Like all satirists but more savagely than any other American satirist except Ambrose Bierce, he delights to dwell upon the discrepancy in the moral world between appearance and reality. He makes this point over and over again. Thus Huck Finn always sees through sanctimoniousness. Thus Twain not once but many times satirizes Sunday-school morality and its accompanying moral tales. Such an exposure is a governing theme in *The Gilded Age, Pudd'nhead Wilson*, and *A Connecticut Yankee*, in short stories like *The Man That Corrupted Hadleyburg* and in many of the essays, as in the instance of Twain's defense of Harriet Shelley, which was published in the writer's lifetime, and "The War Prayer," which was not. Twain has an enormous contempt for the biblical God and for the Bible, both of which he regards as man's invention, an equally enormous contempt for modern Christian governments, a good-natured contempt for most churches and most religions, and a sardonic delight in showing up the difference between official theories of ethics, usually Christian, and the actual motives and conduct of men.

IV

But Twain was also, whether he knew it or not, an eighteenth-century sentimentalist; that is, he really believed that any example of goodness could touch the feeling heart and make men instantly better.

Most of the psychological changes in his stories have the instant quality of Christian conversion. If Twain lacked Rousseau's faith in natural man, he certainly seems to have preferred men in natural environments to men in courts and cities. He looked back with nostalgia upon his life in Missouri, his experience on the Mississippi, his years as a miner, his trip to Lake Tahoe with one companion. Huck Finn and Nigger Jim are two of nature's noblemen as the American claimant in the novel of that name is not—he is merely one of nature's fools. Our author is indulgent toward Colonel Sellers with all his folly, product as that character is of a village culture, but he is merciless upon King Leopold, product of a sophisticated court. True, Twain was also attracted by persons having and exercising power—Henry Rogers, the Standard Oil millionaire, Slade, the murderer in charge of the Overland Express, General Grant, whose moral deficiencies Twain totally neglects. But more important is it to realize that for Twain some human beings totally escape the inglorious human predicament. Such a one was Joan of Arc. Such another was Olivia Clemens. In fact it would be easy to go through his writings and cull out instance after instance of human generosity, saintliness, self-sacrifice, and humility that totally contradict his officially cynical attitude toward altruism. These cases he would be logically forced to categorize as instances of self-deceit, but I find no indication he takes this approach in recording the lives of those he loved and admired. He stood up for the Negro, the Jew, and the Chinaman. One of his favorite adjectives is "noble," and if he often uses it satirically, he also employs it with entire seriousness to characterize a great man or a great action.

Indeed, it is possible to turn my entire analysis upside down—to say that in condemning the Christian God, the Bible, Christian history, the churches, and the Christian world, irascible, passionate, short-tempered, and egotistical as he frequently was, Twain was the foremost Christian of them all. He judged Christianity not by its performance but by its principle. He appealed from Christian fact to Christian idealism. Like Emerson he thought the best thing a Christian could do was to abandon Christianity altogether. Twain's indictment of cruelty, past, present, and to come, is an indictment possible only to a man who truly believes he should love his neighbor, fear God, and keep His commandments. What Twain asked the world was that it permit Christianity to sit in judgment upon Christianity. How else explain at once his gentleness to most children and all animals, his patience with his invalid wife and his unpredictable brother Orion, and his hatred of hypocrisy, his rages against injustice, inhumanity, and war? If he thought the human race ought to be damned or perhaps was already damned, it is still true that damnation is a Christian concept; and it can be argued with great plausibility that Twain's remote cosmic God is no more than an expansion of the God of Job:

> Canst thou bind the chains of the Pleiades,
>   Or loose the bands of Orion?
> Canst thou lead forth the Mazzaroth in their season?
>   Or canst thou guide the Bear with her sons?
> . . . .
> Who then is able to stand before Me?
> Who hath given Me anything beforehand,
>   that I should repay him?

One of the most poignant incidents in all Mark Twain is to be found in *Captain Stormfield's Visit to Heaven,* originally intended as a burlesque on Elizabeth Stuart Phelps's *Gates Ajar.* On his way through space to heaven Captain Stormfield has gone off course to race with a comet, and fetches up at the wrong gate. There he is asked to identify his place of origin. He tries San Francisco, then California, then the United States of America, then the New World, all in vain. He then says he comes from the world, and the angel who is serving as a clerk brusquely replies that there are billions of them. Somewhat humbled, the captain by and by returns and pleads: "I don't seem to make out which world it is I'm from. But you may know it from this—it's the one the Saviour saved." The clerk bends his head gently at the Name, and responds: "The worlds He has saved are like to the gates of heaven in number—no one can count them." Tom Paine, whom Mark Twain often resembles, could not have written this scene. But Paine might have written another sentence by Mark Twain: "To trust the God of the Bible is to trust an irascible, vindictive, fierce and ever fickle and changeful master."

What, then, did Mark Twain think? At some time in the 1880's, if the Paine biography is to be believed, he set down a formal creed in nine successive paragraphs; and though he later departed from many of the several articles, within limits the text gives us the general declaration of faith from which, despite his growing pessimism, Twain did not essentially depart. It begins by stating his belief in the existence of God. It goes on to say that he does not believe God ever sent a message to man by anybody and that He never made himself visible to mortal eyes. Twain thinks the Old and New Testaments were imagined and written by men. Since—and here Twain *is* in line with Tom Paine and Franklin—the goodness, justice, and mercy of God are manifested in His works, Twain thinks they are also manifested to man here now and hereafter. He does not believe in special providences or miracles. He cannot see any value in eternal punishment. He is indifferent about personal immortality. He thinks the moral principles of the world are the outcome of the experience of the world. And he concludes with this striking statement:

> If I break these moral laws I cannot see how I injure God by it, for He is beyond the reach of injury from me—I could as easily injure a planet by throwing mud at it. It seems to me that my misconduct could only injure me and other men. I cannot benefit God by obeying these moral laws—I could as easily benefit the planet by withholding my mud. . . . Consequently I do not see why I should be either punished or rewarded hereafter for the deeds I do here.

If Twain had stuck to this, he would have merely revived the tradition of deism. But with increasing pessimism, the affirmative teleology of the eighteenth century was no longer possible, not merely because of Twain's personal disappointments, but also because developments in science and philosophy made it increasingly difficult to maintain that the earth was made for man.

Twain's pessimism did more than mirror his personal bitterness. It partook of the quality of an important current in late nineteenth-century speculative thought. As Herbert Schneider has said, idealism and agnosticism have been constants in American philosophy; and despite Josiah Royce, despite the Social Gospel, despite populism in politics and the idealism of thinkers like Howison and societies like the Ethical Culture group, the traditional doctrine of inevitable progress in a free democratic society was, in the view of many, overshadowed in the last quarter of that century by despair. The after-effects of the Gilded Age included a growing skepticism about the inevitability of the American dream. The panics of 1873 and 1893 shook men's confidence in business progress, nor were the alternatives presented by anarchism and communism attractive. The American reception of Darwin's *The Descent of Man,* published in 1871, was mixed; but all parties to the controversy it aroused were compelled to admit, explicitly or implicitly, that man was now vastly lower than the angels. Social Darwinism emphasized competitiveness; and though one could argue that evolution meant an inevitable progress in society and perhaps improvement in individuals, the argument was equally plausible that neither church nor state could alter the world of nature, red in tooth and claw. A rugged thinker like William Graham Sumner reduced moral energy to the energy of competing individuals, and in that free-for-all battle the forgotten man was the *petit bourgeois,* the man of good will, the average middle-class American as the average American pictured himself and his world. The assumption that in a closed universe energy dissipates and that modern civilization hastens this dissipation drove both Henry Adams and Brooks Adams into cosmic despair. For them modern life was a struggle between fear and greed in a nightmare out of which, at least for Henry Adams, the only escape was a modern mystique about the medieval Virgin, whom he opposed to the dynamo, which concentrated and exhausted force. In the Harvard yard a group of young poets, among them Edwin Arlington Robinson, George Santayana, and Trumbull Stickney, took refuge in either Schopenhauerian despair, an austere stoicism, or a kind of desperate Epicurean outlook. The vogue in this country of Fitzgerald's version of the *Rubáiyát* of Omar Khayyám was enormous; whole clubs were formed to read it and in a modest way carry out its principle of eat, drink, and be merry, for tomorrow we die. A bitter novel like E. L. Voynich's *The Gadfly*, a tour de force published in 1897, swept through intellectual circles, and by and by was to sell its hundreds of thousands of copies in Russia because it was supposed to represent the death of God. Indeed, it was against the widespread *fin de siècle* spirit that Theodore Roosevelt preached his naïve gospel of physical activity for the sake of physical activity. The mood of the period, or at least this aspect of it, was well expressed by William Vaughn Moody in his poem, "Gloucester Moors," two stanzas of which I shall cite. He compares the earth to a ship and queries:

> God, dear God! Does she know her port,
> Though she goes so far about?
> Or blind astray, does she make her sport
> To brazen and chance it out?
> I watched when her captains passed:
> She were better captainless.
> Men in the cabin, before the mast,
> But some were reckless and some aghast,
> And some sat gorged at mess.
>
> . . . .
> . . . thou, vast outbound ship of souls,
> What harbor town for thee?
> What shapes, when thy arriving tolls,
> Shall crowd the banks to see?
> Shall all the happy shipmates then
> Stand singing brotherly?
> Or shall a haggard ruthless few
> Warp her over and bring her to,
> While the many broken souls of men
> Fester down in the slaver's pen,
> And nothing to say or do?

To this skepticism, this nescience, the idealism of Emerson and the optimism of Whitman had apparently come at last, at least for many sensitive souls. It was not Mark Twain but Henry Adams who wrote:

> For the first time, the stage-scenery of the senses collapsed; the human mind felt itself stripped naked, vibrating in a void of shapeless energies, with resistless mass, colliding, crushing, wasting, and destroying what these same energies had created and labored from eternity to perfect. Society became fantastic, a vision of pantomime with a mechanical motion; and its so-called thought merged in the mere sense of life, and pleasure in the sense. . . . God might be, as the Church said, a Substance, but He could not be a Person.

In the matter of cosmic pessimism Mark Twain was not unique; he was in some sense representative of a whole tendency in religion and philosophy.

John S. Tuckey

Mark Twain's Later Dialogue: the "Me" and the Machine

Although the last period of Samuel L. Clemens's literary work has been regarded as one of despair, there has recently been an increasing recognition of complexities in the later writings. It is true that there is still a rather prevalent notion that Clemens arrived at despair and then, during his last ten or twelve years, substantially remained there—though he was seldom consistent for very long in much else. And it has often been said that the later writings lack significance because their author had lost his belief in the dignity of man and the value of human life.[1] One is likely to find allusions to *The Mysterious Stranger* and to *What is Man?*, such words as "pessimism" and "despair," and perhaps the phrase "the damned human race" (a phrase, incidentally, that no one seems able to document in the writings), and then a rounding off with a facile finis, ringing down the curtain on a supposedly finished Mark Twain. But this notion of a sustained despair is beginning to look like a disposable myth of Mark Twain criticism. Louis J. Budd has observed that Clemens "was less consistent than ever during his last years,"[2] and that while he had "his nihilistic moods," he "kept adding to the confusion with occasional statements of faith."[3] Coleman O. Parsons has noted that Clemens

---

[1]For a balanced discussion of this critical viewpoint, see Edward Wagenknecht, *Mark Twain: The Man and His Work,* 3d ed. (Norman, Okla., 1967), p. 214.

[2]*Mark Twain: Social Philosopher* (Bloomington, Ind., 1962), p. 188.

[3]*Ibid.*, pp. 207–208.

From John S. Tuckey, "Mark Twain's Later Dialogue: The 'Me' and the Machine," American Literature 41. *Reprinted by permission of the Publisher. Copyright 1970, Duke University Press, Durham, North Carolina.*

liked to have two final words "a hopeful and a hopeless one."[4] And it may be added that these expressions of faith and of hope were something more than occasional and random ones. In Clemens's thought they were philosophically based, even as were his more despairing views. For he had not one but two philosophies; or one might say more particularly, two psychologies—the somewhat older positivistic one, already in vogue when he had been maturing, which viewed human beings as mechanisms, entirely the products of their environment, and the newer one, emphasizing the forces of the unconscious and the significance of dreams. And one can find in the writings a continuing dialogue that he carried forward with a growing awareness of the ways in which these two psychologies enlisted his own divided sympathies and convictions. The two psychologies of course had quite different implications concerning the possibilities for human freedom and survival.[5] And the central issue of Clemens's dialogue was one that is still before humanity: whether man is essentially an automated or an autonomous being; whether he is a slavish and perishable mechanism or a free and immortal spirit.

The psychology that regarded the psyche as essentially and entirely a mechanism became, in the terms in which Clemens understood it, his "gospel," the view that he eventually elaborated in *What Is Man?* This view was, so to speak, first in possession of the field, and it was not until the late 1890's, after the just then developing new psychology had begun to come into its own, that he found an alternate position, an actual basis for a more hopeful outlook regarding the human situation. Thus it is especially in the later period that one finds the aforementioned dialogue. That does not, however, mean that it is absent from the earlier writings. For Clemens was intuitively making his own way toward the newer psychology. His work of the 1870's and 1880's shows the long foreground of his interest in dreams, in illusions, and in evidences of special powers of mind such as "mental telegraphy," by which he meant telepathy. In the 1880's he was already following avidly the investigations of the London Society for Psychical Research, as a

[4]"The Devil and Samuel Clemens," *Virginia Quarterly Review,* XXIII, (Autumn, 1947), p. 603.

[5]The differences are probably greater than the deliberately limited approaches of modern psychology (except for the still not generally credited parapsychology) have so far allowed to become evident. See for example William James's observation that, although he hoped to "force . . . materialistic minds to feel more strongly the logical respectability of the spiritualistic position," he intended to keep his "psychology . . . positivistic and non-metaphysical," although this was "certainly only a provisional haltingplace," in *The Principles of Psychology,* authorized edition (New York, 1890; reprinted in 1950), I, 181–182.

regular reader of its publications. Even if he had as yet no adequate basis for a doctrinal formulation of a second position, it appears that he was looking for one. Walter Blair has observed that "for all his talk [as in the paper on determinism that he had read to his Hartford club] about believing man 'merely a machine automatically functioning,' Mark had not been completely converted by his own eloquence,"[6] and that in *Huckleberry Finn* it may be seen that "against all his logic Mark Twain was fighting for a faith."[7] Mr. Blair perceives the same fight going on in some of Clemens's other works of the 1880's. In *A Connecticut Yankee in King Arthur's Court,* for example, Clemens at one point wrote what looks like an authorial intrusion into the Yankee's narrative, a passage expressing both his acceptance of determinism and his desire to fight against it:

> We have no thoughts of our own, no opinions of our own; they are transmitted to us, trained into us. All that is original in us, and therefore fairly creditable or discreditable to us, can be covered up and hidden by the point of a cambric needle, all of the rest being atoms contributed by, and inherited from, a procession of ancestors that stretches back a billion years. . . . And as for me, all that I think about in this plodding sad pilgrimage, this pathetic drift between the eternities, is to look out and humbly live a pure and high and blameless life, and save that one microscopic atom in me that is truly *me:* the rest may land in Sheol and welcome for all I care.[8]

I believe it can be shown that Clemens was still fighting during those late years that have often been considered his time of hopeless resignation. And, since a number of the later works can now be dated with some accuracy, it seems possible to consider more or less sequentially some phases of the battle.

I have suggested that by the late 1890's he was finding more of a basis for opposing his own reluctantly held deterministic position. In an extended notebook entry of January 7, 1898—actually, a short essay of about 1,500 words—he proclaimed that he had "struck upon a new 'solution' of a haunting mystery"[9]—one that he had concerned himself

[6]*Mark Twain and Huck Finn* (Berkeley, 1960), p. 343.

[7]*Ibid.*

[8]Definitive edition, XIV, 150. This edition, used for this and subsequent references to the published works unless otherwise noted, is *The Writings of Mark Twain,* 37 vols. (New York, 1922–1925), hereinafter cited as *Writings.*

[9]*Mark Twain's Notebook,* ed. Albert B. Paine (New York, 1935), p. 348. This passage may also be seen in the holographic notebooks, as well as in typescript copies, in the Mark Twain Papers collection at the General Library of the University of California, Berkeley;

with much earlier when writing "The Recent Carnival of Crime in Connecticut." That story he now regarded as a crude "attempt to account for our seeming *duality*—the presence in us of another *person;* not a slave of ours, but free and independent, and with a character distinctly its own."[10] He went on to consider the new solution: "The French [evidently Pierre Janet and others of the school of Jean Martin Charcot] have lately shown (apparently) that that other person is in command during the somnambulic sleep; . . . but that *you* [i.e., the person awake] have no memory of its acts. . . . To this arrangement I wish to add this detail—that we have a *spiritualized self* which can *detach itself* and go wandering off upon affairs of its own"[11]—a self having a common memory with the waking self, since the latter could remember dreams. "[M]y dream self," he supposed, "is merely my ordinary body and mind freed from clogging flesh and become a spiritualized body and mind, and with the ordinary powers of both enlarged in all particulars a little, and in some particulars prodigiously."[12] Asserting "I do actually make immense excursions in my spiritualized person," he conjectured, "When my physical body dies, my dream-body will doubtless continue its excursions and activities without change, forever."[13] To be sure, his use here of the word "doubtless" suggests not certainty but a need to reassure himself, and the whole passage represents his wishful thinking at least as much as it does his actual convictions. And Albert B. Paine was surely right in thinking that Clemens had already begun to fictionalize the idea when, at the end of the notebook entry, he wrote, "The time that my dream-self first appeared to me . . . it was dressed in my customary clothes."[14] Still, the entry is something more than a pleasing fancy or a warm-up for fiction: it is recognizably a layman's attempt at analysis of the psyche, inspired by what he had been hearing of the experiments and theories of professionals, and one by which he tried to work out a basis for a belief in human survival after death. Having within the past several years lived in Paris, London, and Vienna, major centers for

see Typescript 32(I), p. I.. I am grateful to the Mark Twain Estate for the opportunity to study the notebooks and other materials in the collection, and to Henry Nash Smith and Frederick Anderson for many valuable suggestions. For specific confirmation of the dating of the presently considered passage, which was dated a year earlier by Paine, I here express my thanks to Mr. Anderson and to Howard G. Baetzhold.

[10]*Ibid.*

[11]This passage was published with slight inaccuracies in *Notebook,* p. 349; I have quoted from the Typescript, 32(I), pp. 3–4.

[12]Typescript, 32(I), p. 4; see also *Notebook,* p. 350.

[13]Typescript, 32(I), p. 5; see also *Notebook,* p. 351.

[14]Typescript, 32(I), pp. 6–7; see also *Notebook,* p. 352.

psychological research, he had many opportunities to know of recent developments. But his principal source may have been William James's *The Principles of Psychology,* which Clemens had read and had commented upon in earlier notebook entries.[15] James discusses at length Pierre Janet's work with the subject Léonie, a somnambulist found to have three distinct selves.[16] In other chapters James considers the "spiritual self" and also presents the testimonies of a number of persons whose hallucinatory experiences had been as far-ranging and as remarkable as those Clemens attributed to his dream self, and had seemed as real.[17] And in discussing the perception of reality, he goes about as far as Clemens in recognizing the possible reality of what we call dreams:

> The world of dreams is our real world whilst we are sleeping, because our attention then lapses from the sensible world. Conversely, when we wake the attention usually lapses from the dream-world and that becomes unreal. But if a dream haunts us and compels our attention during the day it is very apt to remain figuring in our consciousness as a sort of sub-universe alongside of the waking world. Most people have probably had dreams which it is hard to imagine not to have been glimpses into an actually existing region of being, perhaps a corner of the "spiritual world."[18]

It is of interest that the notebook passage was written some few months after Clemens had, in August, 1897, been writing the first and most rigorously deterministic part of the existing manuscript of *What Is Man?* It is also interesting that this notebook entry was made at just about the time that he had been composing the first part of *The Mysterious Stranger*—that is, of the "Eseldorf" version that was used for most of the story as posthumously published in 1916. Both sides of the dialogue are represented in the published story, although it is of course the pessimistic "gospel" that chiefly is expressed. It is only in the concluding chapter—which was written for the later "Print Shop" version[19]—that the stranger reveals himself to be the dream self of the narrator. Clearly, when he came to the writing of the "Print Shop" manuscript Clemens meant to explore and assess the relationship of the

[15]Typescript 31(I), pp. 6, 11.
[16]James, I, 385–390 and *passim.*
[17]*Ibid.,* I, 296; II, 114–133.
[18]*Ibid.,* II, 294 n.
[19]The course of composition of *The Mysterious Stranger* and some related manuscripts is discussed in John S. Tuckey, *Mark Twain and Little Satan: The Writing of "The Mysterious Stranger"* (Lafayette, Ind., 1963), pp. 9–81.

dream mind to the other levels of consciousness. In that version there is much about the waking self, the somnambulistic self, and the dream self or immortal self, and these aspects of the psyche are individualized as characters in the story.[20] Clemens was working out what he had envisioned in the note of January, 1898. It is evident that he had not so much taken occasion to do so in the earlier-written "Eseldorf" manuscript, most of which was composed in 1899 and 1900; instead, he made the story an exposition and a fictional portrayal of such pessimistic views as he had advanced in *What Is Man?* It is likely that the dark events of war and of world politics at the close of the nineteenth century prompted him to put aside for a time any extensive following up of the more hopeful implications concerning the human condition and, in the face of seeming fresh proofs that mankind was unworthy of freedom and of survival, draw out the lesson on human worthlessness. But by the time that he was writing most of the "Print Shop" manuscript—in 1903 and 1904—he was no longer under quite so black a shadow: the Boer War, the Spanish-American War, and the Boxer uprising and subsequent military actions in China were past events; the Russo-Japanese War had yet to become a further cause for disillusionment. There were, on the other hand, compelling personal reasons for employing literary strategies that might yield a hopeful answer to the problem of survival. Most of the "Print Shop" manuscript was written while his wife Olivia was in her last illness, and there is some evidence, which I have considered in a monograph,[21] that it was probably at about the time of her death, which came on June 5, 1904, that he wrote, as an anticipated conclusion, the chapter that was used to complete the published story. That chapter does work out at least a minimal survival for the individual—if at the cost of letting all else go to Sheol while preserving his essential self. The boy narrator learns that the world and all of his experiences of it have been "a grotesque and foolish dream," and that he alone exists and will forever "remain a *thought,* the only existent thought, . . . inextinguishable, indestructible."[22] Before dissolving into nothingness, the mysterious stranger reveals that he is merely a projection of the boy's own thought: "I am but a dream—your dream, creature of your imagination." Moreover, *"Life itself is only a vision, a dream."* When his dream self tells him, *"Nothing exists save empty space—and you!"* the lad

[20]Most of the "Print Shop" manuscript remained unpublished until it was published in full in a volume of the Mark Twain Papers: William M. Gibson, ed., *Mark Twain's Mysterious Stranger Manuscripts* (Berkeley and Los Angeles, 1969).

[21]*Mark Twain and Little Satan,* pp. 62–64.

[22]*The Mysterious Stranger, Writings,* XXVII, 138–140.

echoes, "I!"[23] And it is the essential "I" that remains, that is saved. Of course one could suppose that it was again Clemens's hope and not necessarily his firm belief that here found expression. Nevertheless, the conclusion develops great emotional force; furthermore, it amounts to an assertion of a philosophical position, that of an absolute solipsism. Although from a commonsense point of view it is easy to treat such a position as an absurdity, it may be considered a legitimate countering of a view of man as a mere machine in a mechanical universe—a view that may also be made to look absurd enough. Either position appears to leave something out of account if not opposed and corrected by the other. It is not surprising that E. S. Fussell should have found, in *The Mysterious Stranger,* a "tension that Twain could never organize" and "a failure to arbitrate the claims of subjective and objective phenomena."[24] His observations tend to confirm that Clemens had a real commitment to both positions.

It was in the following year of 1905 that the dialogue came into sharpest focus and was carried as close to any final resolution as Clemens would ever be able to bring it. In that year he no longer had any immediate need, in behalf of a loved one, for assurances of the preciousness and permanency of individuals. Yet it was again the problem of survival that he addressed, in a novel that he began almost at once upon settling at Dublin, New Hampshire, on May 20, for a summer of writing. The novel was *Three Thousand Years among the Microbes.* Unlikely as it might seem, there are parallels and linkages between this book and *Huckleberry Finn.* It was in August, 1884, when he had been reading proofs of Huck's story, that he had recorded in his notebook a concept of the human situation that anticipated the microbe story: "I think we are only the microscopic trichina concealed in the blood of some vast creature's veins, and it is that vast creature whom God concerns Himself about and not us."[25] Furthermore, the microbic narrator, a cholera germ, calls himself "Huck," and the human "planet" he inhabits, a chronically drunken and odoriferous tramp named Blitzowski, is reminiscent of Huck Finn's degenerate father Pap. The tramp has other Hannibalesque features. For instance, he contains "many rivers (veins and arteries)" that "make the Mississippi . . . trifling . . . by comparison."[26] And the situation of Huck Finn, who

[23]*Ibid.,* p. 138.

[24]Edwin S. Fussell, "The Structural Problem of The Mysterious Stranger," *Studies in Philology,* XLIX, 104 (Jan., 1952).

[25]*Notebook,* p. 170.

[26]*Three Thousand Years among the Microbes,* in *Mark Twain's "Which Was the Dream?" and Other Symbolic Writings of the Later Years,* ed. John S. Tuckey (Berkeley, 1967), p. 437.

rafts upon the Mississippi, is paralleled by that of the germ "Huck" who journeys in Blitzowski's veins. Moreover, even as Huck Finn is much of the time fleeing from some threat of violence and possible destruction, so is "Huck" the microbe much concerned with the problem of survival. Clemens may be seen improvising various devices that may allow "Huck" to avoid the destruction of his essential "me." For example, it is disclosed that as a microbe he has eternal youth—*almost:* his body is still keeping human time, a week of which lasts for a thousand microbe years; thus while his germ comrades grow old and die, he does not perceptibly age. Of course this stratagem does not actually dispose of death but merely postpones it. But still more hopefully "Huck" finds that with his microbic sight he can distinguish individual atoms, and that each one is an individual, alive and indestructible. And he rhapsodizes that *"there is no such thing as death."* [27] Yet it soon appears that not even these considerations can really provide any lasting reassurance. His atoms will all survive, but will *he?* Reflecting that "D. T. will fetch Blitzy" some time, bringing about the end of the world he inhabits, he muses, "My molecules would scatter around and take up new quarters . . . but where should *I* be? . . . There would be no more *me.*" [28] And he continues his fearful reasonings:

> [M]y details would be doing as much feeling as ever, but I should not be aware of it, it would all be going on for the benefit of those others, and I not in it at all. I should be gradually wasting away, atom by atom, molecule by molecule, as the years went on, and at last I should be all distributed, and nothing left of what had once been Me. . . . And to think what centuries and ages and aeons would drift over Me before the disintegration was finished, the last bone turned to gas and blown away! I wish I knew what it is going to feel like, to lie helpless such a weary, weary time, and see my faculties decay and depart, one by one, like lights which burn low, and flicker, and perish, until the ever-deepening gloom and darkness which—oh, away, away with these horrors, and let me think of something wholesomer! [29]

It seems likely that in writing the latter part of this passage Clemens was imaginatively back in Hannibal, seeing again the fiery death of the hapless drunken tramp who had burned up in the jailhouse one night while the horror-stricken young Sam had watched, remembering

[27]*Ibid.*, p. 447.
[28]*Ibid.*, p. 458.
[29]*Ibid.*

that he had earlier that day provided the man with some matches.[30] His own life may have seemed fatefully linked to that of the tramp, even as was "Huck" the microbe's to that of his tramp-planet Blitzowski. For that matter, the name "Blitzowski" translates as "man of lightning" or "blazing one"—a man afire. Clemens may have been looking full-faced at the most terrible image of death that was in his disaster-laden memory. And at this point the outlook for survival might seem to have perished with the expiring flickers of flame: apparently the "me" could not be saved. Some three days after he had done his last work on the microbe story, he wrote, on June 26, his "Apostrophe to Death":

> O Death, O sweet & gracious friend,
> I bare my smitten head to Thee, & at thy sacred feet
> I set my life's extinguished lamp & lay my bruisèd heart.[31]

One might think that here indeed was the finis to Clemens's hope; that this at least was confirmed resignation. Yet such was still not quite the case. A few days later, on June 30, 1905,[32] he had reread his unfinished "Print Shop" story, for which he had already written the chapter that would immortalize the conscious "I" of the narrator, and was carrying it toward that planned conclusion. He did not quite bring the story through to that point, however, for he put it aside about July 12, after Frederick A. Duneka of Harper & Brothers had visited him to see whether he could provide something for the next winter's book trade.[33] Clearly, *The Mysterious Stranger* was not what Duneka was looking for. Clemens turned to work on "Eve's Diary." But in August he did some further work on *What Is Man?*—and by paper and ink comparisons as well as other evidences the parts he then wrote can be identified. The earlier-written parts are, despite their having been written in the form of a Platonic dialogue, hardly a real dialogue in that only one viewpoint is effectively presented. The Young Man is hardly more than a foil for the mechanistic monologue of the Old Man, the cynical

[30]See *Mark Twain's Autobiography*, 2 vols. (New York, 1924), I, 130–131; also *Life on the Mississippi, Writings*, XII, 455.

[31]In Arthur L. Scott, *On the Poetry of Mark Twain* (Urbana, Ill., 1966), p. 127.

[32]Clemens's marginal note on p. 432 of the "Print Shop" holograph provides this date. For other datings of Clemens's work of the later years I have relied on various evidences such as his correspondence, dictations, notes, and marginalia; internal evidences of successive stages of revision of the manuscripts; paper, ink, and handwriting comparisons of the manuscript materials. In making such investigations I drew heavily upon the expert knowledge and unfailing helpfulness of the Literary Editor of the Mark Twain Papers, Frederick Anderson.

[33]See *Mark Twain and Little Satan*, p. 69.

expositor of determinism. It is in the parts added in 1905 that there emerges, if only briefly, some real dialogue. In a section entitled "A Difficult Question," the Old Man and the Young Man consider "Who is the Me?" And when the crux of the argument is at last reached, it rather astonishingly turns out that the Old Man, who always before has been so sure of his position, is in a state of uncertainty:

> O.M.: . . . You say the mind is wholly spiritual; then you say "I have a pain" and find that this time the Me is mental *and* spiritual combined. We all use the "I" in this indeterminate fashion, there is no help for it. . . . The intellect and the feelings can act quite *independently* of each other; we recognize that, and we look around for a Ruler who is master over both, and can serve as a *definite* and *indisputable "I"* and enable us to know what we mean . . . when we use that pronoun, but we have to give it up and confess that we cannot find him.[34]

And the Old Man makes no effective denial, offers no rebuttal, when his young companion propounds the key question—proposes that which, if true, must discredit the "man is a machine" philosophy:

> Y.M.: Maybe the Me is the Soul?
> O.M.: Maybe it is. What is the Soul?
> Y.M.: I don't know.
> O.M.: Neither does any one else.[35]

And that, it seems, is where we finally come out—with an unresolved dialogue on the unresolved question of the nature and destiny of man. Evidently it was where Clemens himself was still coming out in 1907. His biographer Albert B. Paine has reported his remarks:

> "As to a hereafter, we have not the slightest evidence that there is any—*no* evidence that appeals to logic and reason. I have never seen what to me seemed an atom of proof that there is a future life."

Then, after a long pause, he added:

> "And yet—I am strongly inclined to expect one."[36]

Logic and reason tended to support his "gospel," but there still was a good likelihood that the "me" would escape from the trap of the Old

[34]*What Is Man?*, *Writings*, XXVI, 97–98.
[35]*Ibid.*, p. 98.
[36]*Mark Twain: A Biography*, 4 vols. (New York, 1923), IV, 1431.

Man's logic; that it would turn out to be the Soul. But no certainty, either optimistic or pessimistic, about the matter was attainable in this life. That was clearly still his thought in the last year of his life, when he wrote to Elizabeth Wallace on January 26, 1910, not without some humor:

> Do I "know more" than I knew before? Oh, *hell* no! There was nothing to learn (about hereafters and other-such undesirables), there has never *been* anything to learn and know about those insulting mysteries. I am happy—few are so happy—but I get none of this happiness from "knowing more" of the unknowable than I knew before.[37]

For Clemens, the question of which would finally prevail, the "me" or the machine, was still unresolved—and he was in the last analysis not confirmed in despair, not barred from seeing and representing human life as having value and significance.

---

[37]Samuel L. Clemens to Elizabeth Wallace, January 26, 1910. A copy of this letter is in the Mark Twain Papers. Published in part in Elizabeth Wallace, *Mark Twain and the Happy Island* (Chicago, 1913), p. 137; however, the part here quoted has not been previously published, and for permission to use it I thank Frederick Anderson and the Mark Twain Estate. Copyright © 1969, Mark Twain Company.

Part II

Criticism of the Major Works

Douglas Grant

The Innocents Abroad

The strength of *The Innocents Abroad,* like that of its forerunner, the letters from the Sandwich Islands, lies in its liveliness. The personality of Mark Twain himself and the characters of his fellow tourists, the adventures that befell them and the scenes they visited, are all presented with unflagging high spirits, with occasional wit and a constant appearance of good-humor. The letters were excellent entertainment; there is never a dull moment—at least this is how they were intended to strike the newspaper audience. The need to please such an audience explains in part the obvious vein of facetiousness and vulgarity. The writer tried to chime in with the prejudices and flatter the misconceptions of readers, convinced of their moral, social and political superiority to the Levantine and the European. They were written to be read, and read to national applause. But after all allowances have been made on this score, Mark Twain's own prejudices and misconceptions, at this time too often identical with his readers', and, especially, the sad complexities of S. L. Clemens's character, must be held responsible for the frequently disconcerting tone.

W. D. Howells once remarked, in connection with Twain:

> The West, when it began to put itself into literature, could do so without the sense or the apparent sense, of any older or politer world outside of it; whereas the East was always looking fearfully over its

From Mark Twain, *by Douglas Grant. Edinburgh: Oliver and Boyd; New York: Grove Press, 1962. Reprinted by permission of Mrs. S. J. Grant, Miss A. Grant, and Mr. D. McC. Bell, Executors of the author's Will, and of Grove Press, Inc. Copyright © 1962 by Douglas Grant.*

shoulder at Europe, and anxious to account for itself as well as represent
itself. No such anxiety as this entered Mark Twain's mind.[1]

The remark has wide implications, but considering it as it could be
applied to *The Innocents Abroad,* a plausible excuse is being offered for
the book's tone. If the tone is not personal but regional—and stemming
from a region that has acquired a mythical significance in the development of the American consciousness—then to deplore or even regret it
is to display an unhistorical fastidiousness that blunts the appreciation,
essential in this case, of the candid and independent, but entirely un-
sycophantic and therefore irreverent, spirit of the West. Of course,
Twain shows this spirit, it gives life to the book; and in gratitude for its
invigorating presence, one can forgive it when it only cocks a snook:

> We saw one single coarse yellow hair from Lucrezia's head, likewise. It
> awoke emotions, but we still live.[2]
>
> . . . the rubbish left by the old masters—who are no more, I have the
> satisfaction of informing the public.[3]
>
> I do not think much of the Mosque of St. Sophia. I suppose I lack
> appreciation. We will let it go at that. It is the rustiest old barn in
> heathendom.[4]
>
> The great Rabbi Ben Israel spent three years here [in Tiberias] in the early
> part of the third century. He is dead, now.[5]

But this is not the cause of our uneasiness; it lies much deeper, in the
core of Clemens's being, and can be recognized as fear.

Clemens was frightened. He was frightened by dirt and poverty.
As the tourists walked up the principal street of Horta on Fayal, "these
vermin [the impoverished inhabitants] surrounded us on all sides, and
glared upon us. . . ."[6] And in Naples he noted: "The cholera generally
vanquishes a Neapolitan when it seizes him, because, you understand,
before the doctor can dig through the dirt and get at the disease the man
dies."[7] Of course, as a democrat he deplored the condition of the

[1]"Mark Twain: An Enquiry," 1901, reprinted in *My Mark Twain. Reminiscences and
Criticisms,* New York and London 1910, p. 177. Howells's criticism of Mark Twain is
still the most understanding and illuminating and has been largely drawn on by later
writers on the subject.

[2]*The Innocents Abroad,* New York and London n.d. [1955?], I. 182.

[3]*Op. cit.,* II. 8.

[4]*Op. cit.,* II. 71.

[5]*Op. cit.,* II. 237.

[6]*Op. cit.,* I. 36.

[7]*Op. cit.,* II. 22.

people on good political grounds, but they also frightened him, and he
hid his fear in the harsh, the insensitive jest. And the foreignness frightened him too. All their guides, whatever their names or nationalities,
were "Ferguson": ". . . we called him Ferguson, just as we had done
with all other guides. It has kept him in a state of smothered exaspera-
tion all the time. Yet we meant him no harm. . . . All guides are
Ferguson to us. We cannot master their dreadful foreign names."[8]
Similarly, the Syrian villages are referred to as Jacksonville or Jones-
borough. There is a joke in all this, but a defensive one; the humor is
being used to protect him from what he knows he cannot understand, to
make everyone and everything seem just like home.

Clemens outgrew the last of these particular fears—the first was
gradually consolidated into his wider contempt for the "damned human
race": further experience and maturing sympathies made him readier to
understand and appreciate the world beyond the States—but there are
others in the book which he was never to exorcise. His fear of art, for
example, which in his case, since he was notably lacking in an aesthetic
sense, meant his fear of being taken in. He wandered through the
galleries in a state of angry frustration, refusing to admit that the praises
he heard from all sides were anything but dishonest, preferring the
copies he saw being made to the originals, and deprecating with weak
jokes the masterpieces generally reverenced: "The Last Supper" is
"battered and scarred in every direction, and stained and discolored by
time, and Napoleon's horses kicked the legs off most the disciples when
they (the horses, not the disciples) were stabled there more than half a
century ago."[9] His attitude was thoroughly philistine—and popular;
and yet he could not free himself of the nagging suspicion that he might
be at fault:

> It begins to dawn upon me, now, that possibly, what I have been taking for
> uniform ugliness in the galleries may be uniform beauty after all. I hon-
> estly hope it is, to others, but certainly it is not to me.[10]

This may seem a small matter and not worth the pursuing, but it
must be stressed that the point is not his blindness to the pictures
themselves—it is rather to his credit that he could admit, even facetiously, to "critical imbecility."[11]—but his ridiculing the experience of
art. Whenever he met in others a response determined by emotion,
whether religious or moral or aesthetic, which he himself did not feel,

[8]*Op. cit.*, II. 93–4.
[9]*Op. cit.*, I. 189.
[10]*Op. cit.*, II. 7.
[11]*Op. cit.*, II. 28.

he was tempted to write it down as inane or hypocritical. He was often correct and became expert in cutting through cant, but the human personality at last shrank in the astringent wash of his belittling jokes until his favorite butt was a manikin, not man. And at the bottom of his attitude lay fear: fear of himself—of his own instability and irrationality, of the dark side of his nature, sensitive to the promptings of dread and guilt, the haunt of unwelcome memories and curious dreams. Standing in front of the statue of the flayed Marsyas in Milan, he involuntarily remembered with appalling force how as a boy, after playing hookey from school, he had gone to sleep in his father's office and woken in the night to watch the moonlight steal across the floor to the body of a murdered man:

> I went away from there. I do not say that I went away in any sort of a hurry, but I simply went—that is sufficient. I went out at the window, and I carried the sash along with me. I did not need the sash, but it was handier to take it than it was to leave it, and so I took it. I was not scared, but I was considerably agitated.[12]

Mark Twain's pleasantries save Clemens yet again, and, granted the occasion, one can hardly say at the expense of literature; but he was only to reach his stature as a writer when he was no longer willing to intercede with a joke.

One fear above all can be distinguished running through the related complexities—a fear of sex. It intrudes near the beginning of the book, in the description of the can-can at Paris. He was shocked, both by the dance and the taste that could tolerate it—"I suppose French morality is not of that straitlaced description which is shocked at trifles,"[13]—but yet fascinated by its gusto. His attitude to the can-can—and by extension to the French, for he retained to the end of his life a contempt for them as a people devoted to impropriety ("I even like to look at a Frenchman if I ever have the luck to catch him engaged in anything that ain't indelicate.")[14]—may be explained on moral grounds, but no such excuse will serve in the case of his exceedingly vulgar and absurd narration of the history of Heloise and Abelard. "Such is the history," he concludes,"—not as it is usually told, but as it is when stripped of the nauseous sentimentality that would enshrine for our loving worship

[12]*Op. cit.*, I. 174.
[13]*Op. cit.*, I. 131.
[14]*Extract from Captain Stormfield's Visit to Heaven,* New York and London 1909, p. 107.

a dastardly seducer like Pierre Abelard.''[15] And poor Petrarch and his Laura are as indignantly, and ridiculously, handled. Even the ordinary women he noticed abroad seem to have been too solid to his taste, too decidedly flesh-and-blood. ''Quick, Ferguson! is that a grisette?'' he exclaimed to his guide:

> He showed me dozens of them. They were like nearly all the French women I ever saw—homely. They had large hands, large feet, large mouths; they had pug-noses as a general thing, and mustaches that not even good breeding could overlook; they combed their hair straight back without parting; they were ill-shaped, they were not winning, they were not graceful; I knew by their looks that they ate garlic and onions; and lastly and finally, to my thinking it would be base flattery to call them immoral.[16]

And he was happy to be able to reassure his readers that ''by far the handsomest women we have seen in France were born and reared in America.''[17] The air about them was sufficiently cooled by convention to let him come into their presence without fear.

Mark Twain has earned some reputation, largely on the strength of his ribald—unpublished, though printed—pamphlet, *1601. Conversation, As It Was by the Social Fireside, in the Time of the Tudors* (1880), and reports of his after-dinner conversation, as chafing rebelliously against the taboos of the age, that prevented a frank discussion of sex in print. He did, in fact, complain to Howells: ''Delicacy—a sad, sad false delicacy—robs literature of the two best things among its belongings: Family-circle narratives & obscene stories.''[18] But the remark illustrates only the ease he would have liked to have assumed before the subject, had he not been inhibited by fear. De Voto is unquestionably right in his conclusion: ''I have come to believe that Mark himself was responsible for many of the euphemisms and avoidances which, after due search, can be found in his work, and I am satisfied that the sexual timidities were his.''[19] He was always retreating in his dreams, and in print, to the chaste image of a girlish, a ''platonic sweetheart.''

The tone of *The Innocents Abroad* may be disconcerting to us, however intriguing as a revelation of character, but it scarcely jarred on

[15]*Innocents Abroad*, I. 143.
[16]*Op. cit.*, I. 147.
[17]*Op. cit.*, I. 148.
[18]*Mark Twain-Howells Letters*, Sept. 19, 1877, ed. Henry Nash Smith and William M. Gibson, I, (Cambridge: Harvard University Press, 1960), 203.
[19]*Mark Twain at Work*, Cambridge, Mass., 1942, p. 85.

Twain's readers. They found him a most compatible guide. His fresh
descriptions of scenes interesting in themselves, especially those of the
Holy Land, his soliciting attention by never persisting in a topic but
shifting deftly from the present to the past, from the argumentative to
the ruminative, from places to persons, his bright accompaniment of wit
and humor, his peacock display of personality, and his democratic
determination not to be intimidated by social rank or other pretensions,
made the articles and, later, the book a deserved success.

DeLancey Ferguson

The River

In *Life on the Mississippi* Mark Twain, as always, rearranged his facts for literary effect. He represented himself as considerably younger and vastly more ignorant than he really was in the spring of 1857. But there is no reason to doubt his statements about the lure of the river. For any spirited boy in a river village before the Civil War the steamboat symbolized adventure and romance: an exciting world in itself, and the means to other worlds still more enthralling. A number of Sam's contemporaries had gone on the river; all three of the Bowen boys had become pilots. Obviously Sam had a pretty clear realization that "learning the river" was hard work. But the glory of being a pilot was worth it.

Piloting was a highly skilled profession, and in those days of booming river trade it commanded pay commensurate with the skill it required. A pilot's wages ranged from one hundred and fifty to two hundred and fifty dollars a month, in a world where the purchasing power of the dollar was three or four times what it is today. For Sam Clemens, whose sole acquaintance with large currency had been the fifty-dollar bill which blew his way in Keokuk, such wealth was almost unimaginable. But other aspects of the profession were for him even more alluring than its wages. In that simple society the pilot was the only "unfettered and entirely independent human being that lived on the earth." His orders were obeyed on the run; from his decisions there was no appeal. In his high glass pilothouse, moreover, he was physically conspicuous as well as morally and legally absolute—all of which had boundless attraction for the eternal Tom Sawyer in Sam Clemens. But

Sam Clemens had another side to which the life appealed—his sensitive shrinking from affronts and the crude practical joking that passed for humor—joking which he was still ready enough to indulge in himself, but which hurt and humiliated him when it was practiced at his expense. Even more than the freedom and prestige of the pilot's life, therefore, its security attracted him.

As the *Paul Jones* poked its way down the bankfull river, deeper and deeper into springtime, whatever dreams of the Amazon Sam may have taken with him from Cincinnati faded away. Two hundred miles below Cairo he mustered courage to ask Horace Bixby to take him on as apprentice. The pilot wasn't keen for the job; cubs were a great deal more trouble than profit. After some searching questions, however, he stated his terms: five hundred dollars cash, and the pupil to be responsible for all his own incidental expenses except his board while on the boat—board, by river custom, being free for learners as well as for their masters. Sam hadn't even one hundred dollars, let alone five, but after Bixby had firmly declined to take a few thousand acres of the Tennessee land in lieu of cash they agreed on a hundred down, the balance to be paid out of Sam's first earnings after he got his license. The final sealing of the bargain had to wait until they reached St. Louis on the return trip, when Sam borrowed the hundred dollars from Pamela's husband.

The one phase of Mark Twain's life which needs no retelling is the process of learning the river. To attempt to condense those matchless chapters of *Life on the Mississippi* is futile sacrilege; to quote them *in extenso,* an unwarranted affront to any literate American. From the time Sam embarked on the *Paul Jones* at Cincinnati to his last arrival in St. Louis as a passenger on the *Uncle Sam,* April 19, 1861, was four years, almost to a day. From the literary standpoint they were the four most important years of his life. His own oft-quoted words sum it up: "In that brief, sharp schooling, I got personally and familiarly acquainted with about all the different types of human nature that are to be found in fiction, biography, or history. . . . When I find a well-drawn character in fiction or biography I generally take a warm personal interest in him, for the reason that I have known him before—met him on the river." When he entered on his apprenticeship he was, for all his twenty-one years, and for all that he had been self-supporting since his early teens, still a gawky small-town boy. Those four years made him into a poised and self-reliant man. But some of his experiences marked him for life.

Though in *Life on the Mississippi* he sets the duration of his apprenticeship as two and a half years, he was actually licensed as a pilot on April 9, 1859, a little less than two years after Horace Bixby took him on. He may have piloted freight boats during the last months of his training, for in those simple days fully licensed pilots were legally required only on boats carrying passengers. For Sam those years had included both adventure and tragedy.

A letter to Orion survives which gives a glimpse of the hardships of winter navigation—Sam and his chief out in the yawl for hours, sounding for the channel amid drifting ice that at one time held them trapped until the bow wave of another passing steamboat loosened the floes. When they got back on board they "looked like rock-candy statuary." The boat was the *Pennsylvania,* and Sam's chief at the time was not Bixby but another pilot named Brown (his given name is lacking, even in the casualty lists) to whom Bixby, temporarily engaging in the Missouri River traffic, had committed his cub. Of the mean, tyrannical Brown, and of his Shakespeare-reading copilot, George Ealer, Mark Twain left full-length portraits. But the acrid comedy of Brown's tyranny had a grim ending for Sam.

Henry Clemens had never become the skilled printer that his brother was, and in February 1858 Sam, finding him almost without employment in St. Louis, had helped him to get a berth as assistant "mud-clerk" on the *Pennsylvania.* About three months later came the fight with Brown. The captain had sent Henry to instruct Brown to make a certain landing; Brown, who was deaf but would not admit it, did not hear the order, and later denied that Henry had given it. When Henry next appeared in the pilothouse Brown struck him in the face, and Sam went into action with a fury that must have amazed himself. Brown was the bigger man, but Sam knocked him flat with a stool and then pounded him with his fists while the boat bowled on downriver with no one at the wheel. To interfere with a pilot on duty was the crime of crimes; Sam expected to be put ashore in disgrace at the next stop. But Captain Klinefelter was a just man whose personality shines in one of the innumerable thumbnail character sketches which fill Mark Twain's books. He told Sam, in substance, that Sam had been guilty of a great crime, and that his captain was damned glad of it. But Brown had a lawful grievance; either Sam left the boat, he proclaimed, or he would leave it himself. "Very well," said the captain, "let it be yourself." At New Orleans, however, Captain Klinefelter found no competent pilot available for the return trip and had to retain Brown. So it came about that in mid-June Sam was returning to St. Louis as a passenger on the *A. T. Lacey,* two days behind the *Pennsylvania.*

At Greenville the news was shouted that the *Pennsylvania* had blown up at Ship Island, below Memphis, with the loss of one hundred and fifty lives. From town to town that day the *A. T. Lacey* picked up more news, and before she landed at Memphis Sam knew that Henry was among the dying. He had been blown clear of the wreck, apparently uninjured, but after bravely swimming back to help in the rescue work had collapsed, for the scalding steam had penetrated his lungs. Sam found him with the other hopelessly injured in the improvised hospital at Memphis, and for four days and nights shared the watch by his bedside.

Every detail of the suffering around him burned itself into Sam's mind, and he remembered how, as the thoughtfully screened stretchers bore the dying from the room, a shudder went abreast of them like a wave. From his dying brother's bedside he wrote to his sister-in-law, telling the story of the disaster and hysterically reproaching himself as a hardened sinner who had really deserved all the suffering which was meted out to his innocent brother. And that nothing might be lacking to his morbid self-castigation, there was the torturing possibility that he himself had caused or hastened Henry's death by ignorantly giving him an overdose of morphine.

In one sense Henry's death was the end of his brother's youth. Though his humor and high spirits could not long be quenched, then or in later griefs, his face in repose took on the lined seriousness which for the next twenty years would make him look older than his years, and his mind commenced its endless beating of itself against the unanswerable problems of life and fate. Over and over in his dark moods he would review the Ifs—if he had not quarreled with Brown, if Captain Klinefelter had been able to get another pilot at New Orleans, if he and Henry had not in their last conversation resolved that in case of disaster they would stand by and do what they could, if he had not given that dose of morphine. . . . In this first of the many blows which life would deal him through his affections he first felt the mood of Captain Ahab, cursing the inscrutable malice of the universe which had wounded him.

But meantime life went on. About nine months after Henry's death Sam received his pilot's license and became full partner with his master, Horace Bixby. Much futile ink has been used to "prove" that Sam Clemens was never a good pilot; other ink, equally futile, has been applied to the thesis that his years on the river were the only period of his life when his artistic conscience was at peace, because he was doing the work that satisfied his inward cravings.

On the first point it would seem that no amount of irresponsible river gossip can outweigh the testimony of contemporary records. In 1859 Sam was able to boast to Orion that he was employed while most of the other young pilots were sucking their fingers—employed, moreover, on a good boat at top wages, so that he could bank a hundred dollars a month over and above his expenses—which included substantial contributions to his mother's support and equally substantial "loans" to Orion, who had lost his printing business in the panic of 1857 and was now unsuccessfully engaged in practicing law. (He had been admitted to the bar at Jamestown, Tennessee, in 1858, while living there in one of his many abortive efforts to sell the family land.) He had paid Bixby's tuition fee, and William Moffett's $100 loan. In the following year he gave his mother a spring excursion to New Orleans; the next fall he told of a ten-dollar dinner at a French restaurant. And since just after that dinner he still had twenty dollars to spare for Orion, he must have had steady employment. In that hard commercial and competitive world of steamboating neither Sam Clemens nor anyone else would have continued long at full employment had he not been competent. Nor is there record of any serious mishap to any boat which Sam piloted.

When Albert Bigelow Paine interviewed the aged but still wholly alert Horace Bixby about 1908, the pilot had nothing but good words for the abilities of his most famous pupil and partner. On a later occasion, however, and not for publication, Bixby is reported to have said that "Sam was never a good pilot. He knew the Mississippi River like a book, but he lacked confidence. This developed in him soon after he came on my boat. It never left him. . . . Sam Clemens knew the river, but being a coward, he was a failure as a pilot." It seems reasonable to infer that Bixby was remembering some of the episodes of Sam's apprenticeship. His pupil gave full details, in *Life on the Mississippi,* of the hard and humiliating public lessons by which Bixby taught him to have confidence in his knowledge of the river. Whatever Bixby may have said in 1912, he was not likely to have taken as his partner in 1858 and again in 1860 a man whom he considered a coward.

Yet in a different and subtler way Bixby's statement may well have been true. In 1906 Mark Twain told his biographer, "There is never a month passes that I do not dream of being in reduced circumstances, and obliged to go back to the river to earn a living. It is never a pleasant dream, either. I love to think about those days; but there's always something sickening about the thought that I have been obliged to go back to them; and usually in my dream I am just about to start into a black shadow without being able to tell whether it is Selma bluff, or Hat Island, or only a black wall of night."

. . . .

It is a commonplace of criticism that the two parts of *Life on the Mississippi* are inharmonious, but the reason for the incongruity is not always recognized. The material for the first part of the book was mainly the chapters on piloting which he had contributed to the *Atlantic* in 1874. To complete the first half of the book Mark added three prefatory chapters about the early history of the river, including in them a whole section from the still unfinished manuscript of *Huck Finn* as the best description he could give on the ways of the keelboat and raftsmen. This chapter was never restored to its proper place in the book it was written for. He also added an inferior chapter about cutoffs and the improvident pilot, Stephen, and the three vivid and accurately biographical chapters about Pilot Brown, the *Pennsylvania* disaster and Henry Clemens' death. These completed the narrative of his apprenticeship in the spirit of the earlier work. But this first part remains highly selective in detail and point of view. Its theme is the romance of the river and of piloting; the sordid commercialism of the great days has no more place there than obstetrics or sociology would have in *Tom Sawyer*. Curiously enough, he had nothing whatever to say about his experiences as a licensed pilot. Even with the additional chapters the first half of the book leaves him still a cub. So far as his published writings are concerned, the two years during which some critics suppose him to have been happiest are a biographical blank.

The second half returns to the reportage of the *Innocents* and *A Tramp Abroad*. Though he embroiders and digresses, his primary concern is with things seen and heard, and whether as reporting or as satire, the chapters are notably better than most of *A Tramp*. Three-dimensional characters are present again, as in *Roughing It*— Uncle Mumford, the salesmen of oleomargarine and cottonseed oil, the New Orleans undertaker, the practical joker who tried to feed Mark misinformation about steamboats, they all live and breathe. And though the abundant facts and statistics now have nothing to commend them save a faint historical boredom, the social criticism is still good for a fight south of the Mason and Dixon line.

Mark Twain, Howells thought, was the most desouthernized Southerner he had ever known, and the strongest literary proof of the statement is in this book and in *Huck*. The much-discussed but seldom read chapter that Mark deleted dealt with the postwar attitude of the South toward slavery; it was not nearly so scathing as his published arraignment of Southern ideas of delicacy, refinement, womanhood, religion and propriety, as illustrated by shootings and stabbings performed by Southern gentlemen. He had graduated forever from the roses-and-magnolia legend of the prewar South; what most blunted his criticism, perhaps, was his fondness for seeking a single tangible explanation for, a personal villain behind, any phenomenon he disliked. In this case the villain was Sir Walter Scott. The syllogism was plain: the Southern type of sentimentality, as expressed in print, bore a strong resemblance to the sentimentality of Scott's romances of chivalry. Ergo, Scott was the father of all that Mark disliked in the unrealistic utterances of the South. As a piece of reasoning it was on a par with his later acceptance of the maunderings of the Baconians; straight ridicule of the obsolete verbal flowers, without lugging in Sir Walter, would have been more effective in laughing the fashion out of court.

The weakest part of the book is the interpolated narratives, of which the longest and most labored is the story of the vengeance of Ritter, the Austrian. Later on, when Mark told about the mendacious carpenter in Hannibal, who had filled his boyish ears with yarns about the terrible destruction he wrought upon every man who bore the name of Lynch, he recognized that the man had been talking melodramatic blather, probably borrowed from *Nick of the Woods*. Yet he did not recognize that Ritter's story was precisely the same sort of melodramatic blather, and adding to it a farcical postscript about the treasure which they could not find in the town of Napoleon, because Napoleon had been washed away, did not redeem the situation. But it helped to fill out the book to the contract length, and that was the main consideration.

Henry Nash Smith

Tom Sawyer

I

The germ of *The Adventures of Tom Sawyer* was an unfinished
sketch called "Boy's Manuscript" apparently written in 1870, that is,
during the first year of the writer's married life. This is a literary
burlesque, possibly suggested by David Copperfield's courtship of
Dora. But the comic device of reducing the principals of a story to
children was familiar on the popular stage; even as far west as Carson
City, Mark Twain had seen the R. G. Marsh troupe of Juvenile Come-
dians, whose entire repertory consisted of burlesques of this sort. The
"Boy's Manuscript" translates the story of an adult courtship (possibly
with some reference to Mark Twain's own) into the vocabulary provided by the Matter of Hannibal. Instead of the conventional flower
given by the woman to her lover, Mark Twain's hero, Billy Rogers,
receives from his beloved a piece of molasses candy. He wears it next
his heart until it melts and sticks to him so that he cannot get his shirt
off. Billy Rogers became Tom Sawyer as the book unfolded in the
author's mind, and the original love story was modified somewhat by a
narrative pattern depicting Tom's growth toward maturity. But the childish love affair remains as a central component of what conventional
plot the novel has. Tom's wanderings, intended and actual, are moti-
vated by his despair over being rejected by Becky Thatcher. After their
first quarrel he contemplates suicide, then decides to run away in order

Reprinted by permission of the publishers from Henry Nash Smith, **Mark Twain:**
The Development of a Writer. *Cambridge, Mass.: The Belknap Press of
Harvard University Press. Copyright 1962, by the President and Fellows of
Harvard College.*

to become a pirate, but meets Joe Harper and falls to playing Robin Hood instead. After a later rejection Tom actually embarks on his career as a pirate to the extent of escaping to Jackson's Island with Huck Finn and Joe Harper.

The repetition of plot material in these two sequences suggests that Mark Twain found Tom's amorous experiences deficient in variety and exciting incident. He supplements the burlesque love story with two subplots: the rivalry between Tom and his half brother Sid (which is itself a burlesque of Sunday-school stories about the Bad Boy and the Good Boy), and the melodramatic sequence of events set in motion when Tom and Huck by accident become witnesses of the midnight grave-robbing and Injun Joe's murder of young Dr. Robinson. This material might be one of Tom Sawyer's fantasies except that we are expected to take it seriously. It is another example of Mark Twain's susceptibility to infection from "wildcat literature."

Neither the love story nor the Injun Joe subplot provides a good framework for the Matter of Hannibal, and the rivalry of Tom and Sid serves merely to introduce such boyish crimes as Tom's swimming without permission. Nothing comes of the hint that Sid picks up about the murder of Dr. Robinson from Tom's talk in his sleep. The Matter of Hannibal gets into *The Adventures of Tom Sawyer* primarily through episodes having little connection with the plot. Yet these are the passages for which the book is remembered: the whitewashing of the fence, the Sunday school and church services, examination day at school.

The structural problems of the novel, like those of Mark Twain's earlier books, reflect the instability of his attitudes toward his material. He was not clear in his own mind whether he was writing a story for boys or a story about boys for adults. The burlesque love story presupposes a grown-up audience; it depends for its effect on the reader's perception of the comic parallels between Tom's behavior and that of an adult. Tom's fantasies about pirates and robbers and Robin Hood, again, are relatively meaningless unless the reader can enjoy the ironic contrast between the glamorous fantasy world of romance and the everyday reality of life in St. Petersburg. Both these modes of burlesque interpose a considerable psychological distance between the novelist and his characters, and make it difficult for him to do justice to whatever values may be latent in the Matter of Hannibal. Thus at the end of the whitewashing episode Mark Twain remarks patronizingly that Tom

> had discovered a great law of human action, without knowing it—namely, that in order to make a man or a boy covet a thing, it is only necessary to make the thing difficult to attain. If he had been a great and wise philosopher, like the writer of this book, he would now have com-

prehended that Work consists of whatever a body is *obliged* to do, and that Play consists of whatever a body is not obliged to do.

The incident is reduced to an exemplum illustrating a generalization that has nothing to do with the story. Something tells the writer he is on the wrong track and he confuses things further by mocking at himself.

His uncertain attitude is even more apparent in his efforts to lend importance to the Injun Joe subplot. When the half-breed is found dead of hunger and thirst just behind the iron door Judge Thatcher has had installed at the entrance to the cave, Mark Twain inserts a serious version of Jim Blaine's rumination about special providences, with touches reminiscent of the rhapsody on the Sphinx in *The Innocents Abroad*:

> In one place near at hand, a stalagmite had been slowly growing up from the ground for ages, built by the water-drip from a stalactite overhead. The captive had broken off the stalagmite, and upon the stump had placed a stone, wherein he had scooped a shallow hollow to catch the precious drop that fell once in every three minutes with the dreary regularity of a clock-tick—a dessert-spoonful once in four-and-twenty hours. That drop was falling when the Pyramids were new; when Troy fell; when the foundations of Rome were laid; when Christ was crucified; when the Conqueror created the British empire; when Columbus sailed; when the massacre at Lexington was "news." It is falling now; it will still be falling when all these things shall have sunk down the afternoon of history and the twilight of tradition and been swallowed up in the thick night of oblivion. Has everything a purpose and a mission? Did this drop fall patiently during five thousand years to be ready for this flitting human insect's need? and has it another important object to accomplish ten thousand years to come?

II

The emphasis on Injun Joe's thirst is implausible in view of numerous earlier references to water in the cave; Tom and Becky had encountered him near a spring. Furthermore, such a burst of eloquence is quite out of keeping with the tone of the book. It serves no purpose except to demonstrate that the narrator can produce the kind of associations held in esteem by the dominant culture. The diction of the novel often has a similar effect. Take for example the introduction to the whitewashing incident:

> Saturday morning was come, and all the summer world was bright and fresh, and brimming with life. There was a song in every heart; and if

the heart was young the music issued at the lips. There was cheer in every
face and a spring in every step. The locust trees were in bloom and the
fragrance of the blossoms filled the air. Cardiff Hill, beyond the village
and above it, was green with vegetation, and it lay just far enough away to
seem a Delectable Land, dreamy, reposeful, and inviting.

The elegantly archaic verb form ''was come''; the genteel impersonality
of ''the lips''; ''fragrance'' in place of ''odor''; the literary allusion in
''Delectable Land''; and the telltale reference to dreams, all mark this
as polite prose. The imagery and the tone are intended to establish a
mood of peace and joy as a foil to Tom's ''deep melancholy'' over
being sentenced to whitewash the fence: ''Life seemed to him hollow,
and existence but a burden.'' But the rhetorical effect is overdone.

Another illustration of the psychological distance between the writer and his material is the description of the superintendent's address to
the pupils in the Sunday school, with satirical comments like the following.

When a Sunday-school superintendent makes his customary little
speech, a hymn-book in the hand is as necessary as is the inevitable sheet
of music in the hand of a singer . . . at a concert—though why, is a
mystery: for neither the hymn-book nor the sheet of music is ever referred
to by the sufferer.

The patronizing air is maintained:

The latter third of the speech was marred by the resumption of fights
and other recreations among certain of the bad boys, and by fidgetings and
whisperings that extended far and wide, washing even to the bases of
isolated and incorruptible rocks like Sid and Mary.

In themselves, the witty understatements of ''recreations'' and the
equally witty comparison of Sid and Mary to rocks with waves breaking
against them are amusing, but they represent a kind of exhibitionism on
the part of the writer.

Fortunately, Mark Twain is sometimes able to get rid of his self-
consciousness and render Tom's experience directly, without comment
or moralizing. Such a moment comes during the church service that
follows the Sunday-school scene just quoted. The minister is inviting
the attention of the Almighty to a long list of persons in need of divine
guidance.

In the midst of the prayer a fly had lit on the back of the pew in front
of [Tom] and tortured his spirit by calmly rubbing its hands together,

embracing its head with its arms, and polishing it so vigorously that it seemed to almost part company with the body, and the slender thread of a neck was exposed to view; scraping its wings with its hind legs and smoothing them to its body as if they had been coat-tails; going through its whole toilet as tranquilly as if it knew it was perfectly safe. As indeed it was; for as sorely as Tom's hands itched to grab for it they did not dare—he believed his soul would be instantly destroyed if he did such a thing while the prayer was going on. But with the closing sentence his hand began to curve and steal forward; and the instant "Amen" was out the fly was a prisoner of war. His aunt detected the act and made him let it go.

The language used in describing the fly is easy and effective without being either high or low: it is an almost imperceptible medium of communication. The insect is not a symbol, but the minuteness with which it is described conveys with admirable force Tom's agony of boredom during the prayer. He seizes upon any distraction that offers itself as a relief from his suffering. The austere language in which the fly is depicted is quite different from Mother Utterback's richly colloquial speech. At its best this prose is devoid of vernacular color as well as of all other idiosyncrasies. But Mark Twain could not have achieved such a command of his medium if he had not learned how to free himself from the preoccupation with eloquence that permeated the American literary tradition, and the means of his emancipation had been the skeptical attitude toward ornate rhetoric developed in his repeated exposures of it to comic juxtaposition with vernacular speech.

The description of Tom's secret journey back to St. Petersburg from Jackson's Island is a comparable example of the spare, flat rendering of experience. The series of declarative statements imparts an appropriate forward motion to the prose and engenders a mood of expectancy. Mark Twain carefully refrains from telling us what Tom is about. There is no reason why the information should be withheld except that the writer wishes to fix the reader's attention by something like suspense. Perhaps the result is impressive because it stimulates the inner movement of our feelings in many actual situations: we recognize a strong current impelling us in a general direction, but we do not know what the exact outcome or destination will be. It may be also that stripping away rhetorical ornament fosters vividness by suggesting that the actual situation absorbs all the writer's attention. The passage sounds like Hemingway. Whatever the means by which the effect is achieved, it is an all but complete recapture of the past:

A few minutes later Tom was in the shoal water of the bar, wading toward the Illinois shore. Before the depth reached his middle he was halfway over; the current would permit no more wading, now, so he struck out confidently to swim the remaining hundred yards. He swam quartering upstream, but still was swept downward rather faster than he had expected. However, he reached the shore finally, and drifted along till he found a low place and drew himself out. He put his hand on his jacket pocket, found his piece of bark safe, and then struck through the woods, following the shore, with streaming garments. Shortly before ten o'clock he came out into an open place opposite the village, and saw the ferry-boat lying in the shadow of the trees and the high bank. Everything was quiet under the blinking stars. He crept down the bank, watching with all his eyes, slipped into the water, swam three or four strokes, and climbed into the skiff that did "yawl" duty at the boat's stern. He laid himself down under the thwarts and waited, panting.

Presently the cracked bell tapped and a voice gave the order to "cast off." A minute or two later the skiff's head was standing high up, against the boat's swell, and the voyage was begun. Tom felt happy in his success, for he knew it was the boat's last trip for the night. At the end of a long twelve or fifteen minutes the wheels stopped, and Tom slipped overboard and swam ashore in the dusk, landing fifty yards down-stream, out of danger of possible stragglers.

The information that the current swept Tom downstream faster than he expected lends a peculiar vividness to the passage. Since this had no effect on the outcome of the trip, it does not need to be reported for the sake of logic or coherence. The narrator's remark has the artless, circumstantial air of a witness determined to tell everything he remembers without presuming to judge what is relevant and what is not. The same comment could be made about the statement that the skiff's head stood up high, and the epithet "blinking" applied to the stars: that was the way they looked, although their appearance had no bearing on Tom's mission.

Another moment of almost completely unself-conscious recovery of the past—a moment that must lie close to the emotional center of the Matter of Hannibal for Mark Twain—comes a few pages later, but still in the Jackson's Island sequence:

> After breakfast they went whooping and prancing out on the bar, and chased each other round and round, shedding clothes as they went, until they were naked, and then continued the frolic far away up the shoal water of the bar, against the stiff current, which latter tripped their legs from under them from time to time and greatly increased the fun. And now and then they stooped in a group and splashed water in each other's faces with their palms, gradually approaching each other, with averted faces to avoid the strangling sprays, and finally gripping and struggling till the best man

ducked his neighbor, and then they all went under in a tangle of white legs and arms, and came up blowing, sputtering, laughing, and gasping for breath at one and the same time.

When they were well exhausted, they would run out and sprawl on the dry, hot sand, and lie there and cover themselves up with it, and by and by break for the water again and go through the original performance once more. Finally it occurred to them that their naked skin represented flesh-colored "tights" very fairly; so they drew a ring in the sand and had a circus—with three clowns in it, for none would yield this proudest post to his neighbor.

The language here is again almost without color, but what coloring it has is colloquial. "Whooping" and "prancing" are applied more often to animals than to human beings, and the actions they describe are distinctly indecorous. "Round and round" belongs to colloquial rather than exalted diction, and so does "chase" in the sense of "pursue." (One would prefer, incidentally, to omit "latter" in the last clause of the sentence.) "Averted faces" is somewhat literary in place of "faces turned away," but "ducked," "sputtering," "sprawl," and "break for the water" are drawn from a basic oral vocabulary. The writer is directing more attention to his subject than to his diction; it subordinates itself to the actions described.

As in the description of the fly, the minute detail with which the scene is rendered gives it an air of meaning more than it seems to on the surface. The lavish particularity testifies to the value the author attaches to what he is describing. It would never have occurred to Mark Twain to say that natural facts are symbols of spiritual facts, but the memory of such a frolic had for him thirty years later a significance comparable to what Emerson tried to express in metaphysical terms. Although the value is perhaps too deeply buried ever to be brought to the surface and given precise statement, it is value just the same, and it is not derived from the sources or supported by the sanctions acknowledged in the traditional culture. In contrast with the revulsion against the body implicit in the notion of refinement or ideality, this scheme of values lays stress on sensory experience—of sunlight, water, bodily movement, and physical contact with other human beings—and on impulse rather than schedules as a guide to behavior.

III

The images of Tom in church or Tom whooping and prancing along the sand bar remain in the reader's mind after Mark Twain's struggles with plot and subplot and point of view are forgotten. They belong to his primary alphabet of symbols. Their importance for his subsequent career requires us to examine them with care.

Tom is a kind of embryonic Everyman. In church and school he confronts institutions that seem to him alien and at times hostile; on Jackson's Island he enjoys comradeship with his fellows and he responds to the physical environment. Natural man beleaguered by society, but able to gain happiness by escaping to the forest and the river: this is undoubtedly an important aspect of the meaning that thousands of readers have found in the novel. In situations of this sort nineteenth-century writers were likely to be led by the heritage of Romantic thought to identify themselves with the virtuous hero and to ascribe evil exclusively to society. The signs of such a tendency on the part of Mark Twain himself can be discerned in *Tom Sawyer*. But the church and the school are not truly evil, they are merely inconvenient and tedious; Tom doesn't really intend running away for good; his playing pirate is a child's fantasy, and can with perfect appropriateness have its climax in the boys' return:

> Suddenly the minister shouted at the top of his voice: "Praise God from whom all blessings flow—SING!—and put your hearts in it!"
>
> And they did. Old Hundred swelled up with a triumphant burst, and while it shook the rafters Tom Sawyer the Pirate looked around upon the envying juveniles about him and confessed in his heart that this was the proudest moment of his life.
>
> As the "sold" congregation trooped out they said they would almost be willing to be made ridiculous again to hear Old Hundred sung like that once more.

Here Tom is fully integrated with the community (which is identical with the congregation in the church); the community is completely harmonious within itself; and the general exultation finds expression in the singing of a Christian hymn at the command of the minister. The official culture of St. Petersburg could hardly receive a more absolute affirmation.

It is the absence of a basic conflict between Tom and the society of the village that obliges Mark Twain to look elsewhere for the conflict he considers essential to the plot of a novel. He solves his problem by introducing evil in the form of Injun Joe, whose mixed blood labels him an outsider. Tom and Huck fear him, and Tom is sufficiently aggressive to testify against him in court, but a direct collision is out of the question and Injun Joe has to be destroyed unintentionally by Judge Thatcher when he seals up the mouth of the cave.

While acknowledging, at least tacitly, the artificiality of this sub-plot, Bernard De Voto emphasized its importance in contributing to *Tom Sawyer* "murder and starvation, grave-robbery and revenge, terror and panic, some of the darkest emotions of men, some of the most terrible fears of children." He believed such materials were an important aspect of the book's fidelity to human experience. It is an idyll, he pointed out, but it is enclosed in dread; and this keeps it true to the world of boyhood. The argument has weight. Yet a melodramatic villain tends to evoke a melodramatic hero, and Mark Twain does not entirely resist the temptation. He evades the naïve moral categories of the Sunday-school books by making Tom a boy who is "bad" according to their standards yet "good" according to more profound criteria. The demonstration, however, is not enough to give Tom real depth of character. The reader is evidently meant to see Tom's badness as nothing more than endearing mischief, indicative of a normal amount of imagination and energy; it is not bad at all. Mark Twain has written the Sunday-school story about the Good Little Boy Who Succeeded all over again with only a slight change in the hero's make-up and costume.

If the Matter of Hannibal is to be explored by means of a plot involving a protagonist of this sort, two basic situations are possible. We may have the naturally good hero enjoying a triumphant and harmonious relation with his society (Tom in church while the Doxology is being sung), or the naturally good hero at odds with his society (Tom suffering during the minister's prayer). The first of these alternatives could yield nothing except an endorsement of conventional values. The second alternative was more promising; it at least offered a built-in conflict and a point of view adapted to satire of existing institutions. But *Tom Sawyer* shows how dangerous the idea of a hero's natural goodness was as literary material. It constantly threatened to become merely a stereotype because of the difficulty of imagining a kind of goodness basically different from that endorsed by the accepted value system. Francis Parkman, for example, wishing to praise his French-Canadian guide across the plains, Henry Chatillon, said he had a "natural refinement."

Mark Twain would ultimately need a hero more hostile toward the dominant culture than Tom Sawyer was—Tom, the devotee of the "rules," the exponent of doing things by the book, the respectable boy who took out his impulses toward rebellion in harmless fantasies of escape. It is appropriate that *The Adventures of Tom Sawyer* ends with Tom made wealthy by the treasure he has found, acclaimed as a hero, and basking in the approval of both his sweetheart and her father. His last act is to persuade Huck to return to the Widow Douglas' and be "respectable." No doubt this wind-up of the plot was dictated by "the exigencies of romantic literature'' which Mark Twain later said accounted for the death of Injun Joe in the cave. In the brief Conclusion he almost explicitly confesses that the conventions of the novel as he has adopted them in *Tom Sawyer* have proved to be poorly suited to his materials.

This perception was probably aided by the fact that even before he had finished the book he had recognized the solution for several of his technical problems. It lay in using Huck Finn as a narrative persona. The outcast Huck was far more alienated than Tom from conventional values. Telling a story in Huck's words would allow Mark Twain to exploit fully the color of vernacular speech. At the same time, the use of a narrator who was also a principal actor in the story would virtually compel the writer to maintain a consistent point of view.

In a fashion that recalls Cooper's discovery of unexpected possibilities in Leatherstocking while he was writing *The Pioneers,* Mark Twain seems to grow suddenly aware of Huck's potential importance only a few pages before the end of *Tom Sawyer*. Huck performs his first significant act in Chapter 29 by giving the alarm to Mr. Jones and his sons, who frustrate Injun Joe's plot against the Widow Douglas. The conversation between Huck and the Joneses is reported at surprising length. Mark Twain has evidently become interested both in the workings of Huck's mind and in his speech; he exhibits him in the process of inventing a cover story—an activity that would become almost compulsive in *Adventures of Huckleberry Finn*. Huck's impulse to run away when he learns that the townspeople have gathered to honor him and Tom in a great civic ceremony and his sufferings under the regimen imposed on him by the well-intentioned Widow Douglas are not merely prophetic of the sequel, they merge imperceptibly with the opening chapters that Mark Twain would begin to write as soon as he finished *Tom Sawyer*. Indeed, Tom figures too prominently for the taste of most readers in both the opening and the closing chapters of the later novel. But the differences between the two books—aptly illustrated by the contrast between the tone of the chapters of *Huckleberry Finn* in which Tom appears and the tone of those in which he does not—greatly outweigh the similarities. *Tom Sawyer* provides relatively little opportunity to deal with the problem of values to which Mark Twain had devoted so much attention in his early work; *Huckleberry Finn* is his major effort in this direction.

A. E. Dyson

Huckleberry Finn *and the Whole Truth*

I

. . . "How could he?" we wonder, as we move towards the end of *Huckleberry Finn*. It is not only that our sense of Jim's dignity is outraged as he is sacrificed to Tom Sawyer's nigger-minstrel antics, nor is it merely reluctance to concede that Huck's exquisite sense of values, tested and proved throughout the novel, can fail once more before Tom's adolescent and unreflecting romanticism. What worries us most of all, I think, is the suspicion that a great work of art is being sold out to a schoolboy sense of fun. Tom himself might conceivably turn Jim's predicament into a farce. He hasn't lived through the experience of the raft, morally he is less sensitive than Huck. He knows, moreover, that Jim is already freed, so that his attitude is at least understandable in human terms. But how can Huck and Jim accept the situation as they do? How, above all, can Mark Twain? We look back at that most famous and disregarded of warnings from writer to reader at the beginning ("Persons attempting to find a motive in this narrative will be prosecuted; persons attempting to find a moral in it will be banished; persons attempting to find a plot in it will be shot"), and wonder.

The ending has not, however, lacked its distinguished defenders. T. S. Eliot and Lionel Trilling have both found the return from Huck's world to Tom Sawyer's structurally appropriate. "It is right," says Eliot, "that the mood of the book should bring us back to the beginning"; "A certain formal aptness," comments Trilling. Leo Marx, in an interesting recent essay, has taken them both to task for this. What really counts in a novel, he thinks, is not structural but moral appropriateness, and in this the end of *Huckleberry Finn* is lacking. It is here that I tend for my own part to differ from him, as to some extent from all the critics I have read on the work. Lionel Trilling's general moral claim for *Huckleberry Finn* is that it tells the truth, and to my mind this claim extends to the ending not in the somewhat desultory way he suggests, but as part of the logic and texture of the whole book. The raft, paradoxically idyllic though life on it seems, has to tie up somewhere; and if one honestly favors the whole truth, the return to land at the end, with its lessening tension and its gradual descent from clear-cut decencies and responsibilities to the more muddled ones of everyday life is the only ending that will really, over a long period, ring true.

But this is to jump ahead: best to start, perhaps, from the irony, which is the clearest clue to Mark Twain's intentions that we have, providing a far firmer unity for the work than it gets from the pleasantly picaresque and rambling plot. Twain's sense of the incongruous rubs shoulders with the practical joke at many points, but it also ranges through much of the spectrum of irony, sometimes seeming most at home as it approaches the tragic. "Everything human is pathetic," as Twain himself once wrote. "The secret source of humor itself is not joy but sorrow. There is no humor in heaven." Ernest Hemingway, taking his cue perhaps from this, has gone to the extreme of seeing *Huckleberry Finn* as a novel moved by its own powerful insights in one direction, and wrested away again only by the deliberate sabotage of the author. "If you read it," he says, "you must stop where the nigger Jim is stolen by the boys. This is the real end. The rest is cheating." Yet the true state of affairs, I believe, is that Mark Twain followed the fluctuations of human fortune more subtly than this or any similar view allows. His irony approaches both the comic and the tragic, as most truly great irony does, but it finally rests in neither. Its essential insight can be more usefully linked with the "whole fortune" of Huck and his father, as Jim tells it at dead of night, using a hair ball out of the fourth stomach of an ox.

> Yo' ole father doan' know, yit, what he's a-gwyne to do. Sometimes he spec he'll go 'way, en den agin he spec he'll stay. De bes' way is to res' easy en let de ole man take his own way. Dey's two angels hoverin' roun' 'bout him. One uv' em is white en shiny, en t'other one is black. De white one gits him to go right, a little while, den de black one sail in en bust it all up. A body can't tell, yit, which one gwyne to fetch him at de las'. But you is all right. You gwyne to have considable trouble in yo' life, en considable joy. Sometimes you gwyne to git hurt, en sometimes you gwyne to get sick; but every time you's gwyne to git well agin.

Mark Twain, like Jim's hair ball, responds to life as a gamble, with good and bad endlessly struggling together, neither actually winning, but neither cancelling the other out. The two angels hover, and there is no telling which will come to fetch us at the last. The fate of Huck's father is dubious, but Huck himself? If he takes the rough along with the smooth all will be well with him, though death in one form or another will be waiting at the last. As a philosophy of life we are normally inclined, I believe, to think of such ideas as naïve, and one of Twain's triumphs is to show how much better they stand up to actual experience than the more sophisticated beliefs of Miss Watson and the widow. Throughout *Huckleberry Finn* good and evil are shown co-existing in Nature as well as in man. The squirrel Huck sees as a natural friend, the snake as a natural enemy: why?—because the one he can live with, embracing its faults with his tolerance, and the other he can't. There is an acceptance of fact here which is not only part of Huck's unsentimental common sense, but part too of the common sense of Mark Twain himself manipulating the irony. Most human minds gravitate towards either optimism or pessimism; there is a constant temptation to think that either good or bad will "win" in the end. Mark Twain, like Huck, does not share this view—which is why his irony never settles in either a comic or a tragic mould, and why his ending is deliberately less conclusive than either would require.

Doubts about the ending of *Huckleberry Finn* cluster around another misconception, not dissimilar to the one of Hemingway I have been considering. This is the very common error of regarding the novel as a simple contrast between *two* worlds—the one civilized, insensitive and corrupt, the other uncivilized, sensitive and humane. The widow, "dismal, regular and decent" as Huck calls her, is seen as typical of the former, Huck himself and Jim as typical of the latter. Tom Sawyer, while having many fine qualities, belongs basically to the widow's world; and Twain's irony is taken to be the playing off of the genuine against the conventional, the good, if one likes, against the bad.

Now though this is true in that the values achieved on the raft are used for an ironic survey of society at large, I am convinced that to put the matter so simply is misleading. For one thing it overlooks, as most criticism does, the importance of the Duke, the King and Huck's father. These are all much further from the "respectable" folk than Huck himself is, yet they are the most decisively evil characters in the book. One has only to recall them to be aware that Jim stands less hope of mercy from this group than he does from Miss Watson and Tom, and that a straight choice of "outsider" against "insider" is not at all what is being presented. Nor is this all. The eventual freeing of Jim comes

about not through the journey on the raft, but through a change of heart
in his former owner. The method by which it happens is muddled, the
insights behind it are less pure, to put the matter mildly, than those of
the raft, yet the fact of freedom comes from Miss Watson's dying
request, and from the camp of the respectable. In allowing this, Mark
Twain is not "selling out" the rest of the novel, as some commentators
assume, but simply being faithful to the realism which makes us trust
him all along. Respectable morality, though muddled and sometimes
cruel, does have certain ideals behind it: the ideals, indeed, which Huck
himself embodies in a purer form, outside society, and paradoxically in
defiance of it. The world of the widow and of Miss Watson might be
blinkered, and provided with blind eyes for all occasions; it might recoil
with horror from its own more Christian ideals when despite every
precaution it catches sight of them. But it is myopic rather than totally
blind, thoughtlessly rather than willfully cruel. Miss Watson's request
in her will is the beginning, maybe, of a challenge to the system of
slavery from inside; a moment without which no purer moral protest,
however noble, would stand much hope of eventually winning the ma-
jority to its side. If we think historically, we shall see that her dying
decision to free Jim, despite the fact that he has sinned both against
herself and against the economic system by escaping, may be as important a landmark on the road to emancipation as the dangerous quest for
freedom on the raft itself. Actual humane progress does come about,
whether we like it or not, through muddled insights, muddled kindli-
ness, muddled actions as much as from the straightforward vindication
of ideals. Twain's ending draws attention to this, too, and it is part of
the whole truth he has to tell.

At the end, the values of the raft are assimilated to the pattern of
life seen steadily and as a whole. Could Mark Twain really have shown
Huck and Jim simply winning through to freedom, without violating
history and contriving an ending we should have doubted? Could any
conceivable ending, on the other hand, have really betrayed the realities
of the raft, in such a way that we should retrospectively doubt them?
The final balance is one in which we see what has been achieved on the
raft as real rather than illusory, yet exceptional rather than normative.
And this, I am sure, is what the author intended.

For consider the journey itself. During the course of it, Huck and
Jim are living in a very special world, from which almost all the distinc-
tive data of human living have been removed. There is no sex on the
raft, no politics, no formal worship, no money, no status. There are no
traditional sanctions, either. Huck is unimpressed by dead people, including Moses; even his Conscience turns out to be a Trojan Horse

smuggled in by the enemy, not a genuine moral inheritance from the past. There is, however, in this apparent vacuum, and in the strenuous business of survival which occupies it, a fundamental human decency at work which is the ground for all good manifestations of sex, politics, worship, money, status, wherever they occur. In being driven outside society, Huck and Jim are given an occasion to transcend it. Their tenderness and affection for one another is the condition of all good relationships, private or public; their sensitivity to the grandeur and mystery of nature and to the suffering of men is the condition for all true reverence; their deep sense of responsibility, and their natural dignity, are a condition for all uses of money and status that can ever deserve respect. In the world of the raft, they represent a type of pre-morality; a decency outside civilization, which is both a seed for all that grows good inside it, and a touchstone for all that turns bad. To achieve the raft, Huck has to renounce everything—his father, his money, even his official life; Jim, to achieve it, has to be betrayed even by his owner, and to be driven to complete isolation. In the ensuing events, totally exiled from humanity, the two of them achieve the highest type of relationship of which humanity is capable. The paradox involved in this is not overlooked; it is, indeed, the impetus of much of the irony. Yet Huck and Jim are not mistaken for, or presented as, a norm. Their morality cannot exist permanently without social contexts, and when it returns to these it will be unable, perhaps, to exist as purely and unambiguously as it does on the raft. At the end, they return to the world where their values, never articulate at the best of times, will become clouded again by the mesh of actuality. When this happens, the raft will remain as a memory, and as a leaven. And this, in fact, is what happens. We are left with the assurance that there is, in man, a power for good as well as bad and that good is worth fighting for; we are not left with the assurance that the power for good is normally or easily followed, or that it will necessarily win.

II

But at this point we must approach Mark Twain's irony more directly. At one end of the scale, as we know, there are the practical jokes—the simple incongruities of fooling people which are usually associated with Tom Sawyer, though Huck can be his uneasy partner at times. Tom Sawyer has often been called a "romantic," and so he is, if one uses the word to mean, not necessarily with disrespect, the adolescent and the immature. In a fairly obvious way, he is a distinguished

example of a type familiar in British boys' books of the period-
—healthy, good-natured, full of animal spirits, a born leader of men.
He flirts with the terrible as he does with Becky Thatcher, courting
death and glory without being entirely aware of what he is doing, and
without therefore being entirely serious. His immaturity is ironically
underlined, yet Mark Twain sympathizes with Tom in important ways.
He likes his boisterousness, his courage, his lively fancy, his sentimentality, his *joie de vivre*. Tom is the sort of lad that Dr. Arnold would
also have been happy with at Rugby; a Christian boy?—hardly; a Christian gentleman?—yes, given time, that is just what he will be. His
unreflecting, limited but not uncostly decency is a pre-eminently respectable virtue; unlikely, as Huck knows, to engage in such eccentric
enormities as nigger emancipation, especially at this stage of history,
but to be relied on nonetheless for goodwill to all men insofar as expe-
diency and the general good permit. His immaturity is of the type
which, properly nurtured, passes unscathed through adolescence into
manhood, protecting the ruling class by and large, with all its gifts, its
virtues and its opportunities, from producing too many radicals, intellectuals, artists and others disruptive of the *status quo*. He is a good
empire-building type; an adventurous extrovert, as Mark Twain himself
was; far more fit than Huck to be running the world, and far more likely
to be doing so. Even his naughtiness exists, as one critic has pointed
out, only inside the limits that he knows are expected of him. And his
make-believe, like his jesting, goes to show that though his fancy is
lively, his imagination—and especially his moral imagination—is dul-
led and conventional. Moral imagination—the response to people and to
events with direct insight and sympathy—is exactly, of course, the
quality in which Huck excels. This is why Huck is never wholly at ease
with Tom, though he naturally looks up to him. It is also why Huck is
peculiarly fitted to see the deepest moral truths, though he is at the same
time peculiarly unfitted to articulate them, or to set about making them
prevail.

Practical joking, and its implications, is only the start of our enquiry. Mark Twain's sense of the discrepancies between one world and
another goes beyond the gulf between schoolboy fantasy and reality; the
more basic gulf between Tom and Huck is the clue that leads towards
the heart of the matter. Consider, for example, the following passage, in
which two essentially adult worlds are held in sharp contrast.

> Then Miss Watson she took me in the closet and prayed, but nothing
> come of it. She told me to pray every day, and whatever I asked for I
> would get it. But it warn't so. I tried it. Once I got a fish-line, but no
> hooks. It warn't any good to me without hooks. I tried for the hooks three

or four times, but somehow I couldn't make it work. By and by, one day, I asked Miss Watson to try for me, but she said I was a fool. She never told me why, and I couldn't make it out no way.

I set down, one time, back in the woods, and had a long think about it. I says to myself, if a body can get anything they pray for, why don't Deacon Winn get back the money he lost on pork? Why can't the widow get back her silver snuffbox that was stole? Why can't Miss Watson fat up? No, says I to myself, there ain't nothing in it. I went and told the widow about it, and she said the thing a body could get by praying for it was "spiritual gifts." This was too many for me, but she told me what she meant—I must help other people, and do everything I could for other people, and look out for them all the time, and never think about myself. This was including Miss Watson, as I took it. I went out in the woods and turned it over in my mind a long time, but I couldn't see no advantage about it—except for the other people—so at last I reckoned I wouldn't worry about it any more, but just let it go. Sometimes the widow would take me on one side and talk about Providence in a way to make a body's mouth water; but maybe next day Miss Watson would take hold and knock it all down again. I judged I could see that there was two Providences, and a poor chap would stand considerable show with the widow's Providence, but if Miss Watson's got him there warn't no help for him any more. I thought it all out, and reckoned I would belong to the widow's, if he wanted me, though I couldn't make out how he was a-going to be any better off then than what he was before, seeing I was so ignorant and so kind of low-down and ornery.

The irony here is not generated by Huck's conscious attitude. When he sees through people himself, as he often does, it is only after "thinking it all out," and then with a shrewd and charitable insight far removed from any tone that would lead to irony, or that an ironist himself could adopt. Though Huck tells the story, in other words, the irony comes directly from the author behind Huck; it is a communication to the reader in which the narrator has no share. Where, then, is the irony aimed? Are the widow and Miss Watson its targets? To some extent, yes; their piety is unreflecting, and their dealings with Huck are less than intelligent. Yet they mean well, as Huck correctly allows, and their belief in prayer and in Providence is not entirely discredited, though it is damaged, by Huck's reflections. Might the irony, then, be at the expense of Huck? On a superficial reading we are tempted to think so, and it is here that Mark Twain's most basic moral trap exists for the reader: if we think that Huck is the victim, we are in fact the victims ourselves. For Mark Twain is neither here nor elsewhere a civilized man glancing with superior amusement at ignorance—his is not the irony of a Gibbon, or a Lytton Strachey; nor is he an indulgent father smiling at the errors of a favorite child—still less is it the irony of

a Lamb. Though at first sight Huck's reasoning is deceptively school-
boyish, a moment's reflection reveals not its folly, but its wisdom. For
one thing, he pays the widow and Miss Watson the compliment of
taking them seriously, even though what they say sounds to him like
nonsense. He has the humility and readiness to learn without which any
education, however sophisticated, cannot be more than a sham. But
then again, he has shrewdness and independence of judgment, the qualities which are at the root of his remarkable moral honesty and intelligence. Testing what he has been told against his own experience of life
and his own observation of people, he finds grave reasons for doubting
it. These doubts are anything but ill-informed cynicism; they have a
seriousness which places the traditional piety of Miss Watson and the
widow very exactly, and it must be admitted very damagingly, for what
they are. Huck's own "religious" awareness is governed by things he
knows—the mysterious grandeur of the river, the stars in the night sky,
the age-old folk-lore of good and bad omens, which fit in with his sense
of the splendors and uncertainties of life better than doctrines of prayer
that he can't make to work, and tales of Providence, Heaven and Hell
that relate to no experiences he has had.

Huck is serious and honest, then; he is also kind and gentle. It is
these latter qualities which make the word "wisdom" rather than
"common sense" seem appropriate. He is sure that Miss Watson and
the widow are doing their best to educate him, and he has no wish to
hurt them by arguing. Whenever he can, he gives them the benefit of the
doubt. Prayer does work, perhaps, for some folk, but not for the likes of
him. This possibility he accepts unselfconsciously and without bitterness. The fact that he does so is part of the irony, but his obtuseness at
this level, unlike that of (say) Gulliver, reflects nothing but credit on
himself.

What one sees in this passage, more than anything else, is Huck's
selflessness and humanity, all the richer for the paradoxical form they
take. For though he applies tests of self-interest to prayer and Providence, and is quick to see that Miss Watson herself is less disinterested
than she might think, it is his good sense, not his greed, that is proved.
His real selflessness can be easily seen in the readiness with which he
accepts himself as "low-down and ornery" without, however, making
this an excuse for bitterness or irresponsibility, and in the fine natural
courtesy towards others which he invariably has. A similar important
paradox inheres in his lies. "I never seen anybody but lied, one time or
another," he comments, but his own lies are always related to a deeper
honesty: fidelity to fact and to good sense as he sees them. His lies, are,
in fact, worked out in the face of much he is asked to believe, evasive
action taken not because he is willful or stupid, but because he is

generous and alive. They are a technique for surviving in a largely immoral world with as little unpleasantness for himself and for everyone else as possible. Jim, who shares Huck's predicament, shares his attitude to lying. His greeting to Huck when he first meets him during the escape, and thinks he must be a ghost, is a splendid example of the type of lie which includes in almost equal measure an instinct for survival, a deference to fact however unexpected, genuine courtesy even to one as beyond the pale as a ghost, and a sense that one outcast ought to be able to appeal to the sympathy and goodwill of another, even if naked truth isn't wholly expedient. "Doan' hurt me—don't! I hain't ever done no harm to a ghos'. I alwuz liked dead people, en done all I could for 'em. You go en git in de river agan, whah you b'longs, en doan' do nuffin to Ole Jim, 'at 'uz alwuz yo' fren'."

What, then, characterizes this irony most? It does not score points against people as its main aim, and is wholly untainted with the assumption of superiority. At root, it is a juxtaposing of two or more real worlds at points where they do not, and cannot, meet. Both worlds exist, and though Huck's is the more virtuous, that of Miss Watson and the widow is the more usual. The irony offers a rich realism, the "whole truth," as I am calling it; but the whole truth shot through with a moral awareness without which such a description of it would not be deserved, and with a charity rare among writers who use irony at all.

III

The inevitable question concerning Mark Twain's values now presents itself. How far is *Huckleberry Finn* the expression of a clear preference, either for radicalism or for the noble savage? The answer is not clear-cut. If one tries Mark Twain out with some radical causes of the present day, he can sometimes seem reactionary. He would have been anti-apartheid, of course; if his irony is committed to any obvious "cause" it is that. But he might well have been for hanging rather than against it, on the familiar grounds, abundantly clear in his work, that reformers interested only in kindness overlooked the grim realities of human evil, against which society must protect itself strongly, even ruthlessly, to survive. Huck's charity, it is true, transcends this, by way of an equally ruthless honesty on the other side. Confronted with the murderers trapped on the boat, he reflects: "I began to think how dreadful it was, even for murderers, to be in such a fix. I says to myself, there ain't no telling but I might come to be a murderer myself, yet, and then how would I like it?" And when the Duke and the King have perpetrated every possible treachery against both himself and Jim, he can still spare them compassion in their own misery and suffering. But Mark Twain himself, on the whole, feels that murderers and others like them deserve what they get; as to the do-gooders like the new judge who thinks he can reform Huck's father by kindness, they come in for frequent satiric treatment at his hands.

Mark Twain takes evil seriously, in other words, and he believes that strong social law is necessary to combat it, even though law will be tainted with the defects of the class who make it. This becomes more obvious when one thinks of the really anti-social figures in *Huckleberry Finn*. Huck's father, the Duke and the King are all failures, who stand outside society not because they are too honest for it, like Huck, or unjustly discriminated against by it, like Jim, but simply because they are lazy, vicious, and by nature parasitic. The passage in which Huck's father fulminates against the Government for tolerating an educated "nigger" is irony of the straightforwardly boomerang kind, and of him, as of the other scoundrels in the book, there is no good to be said. Though Huck understands and pities them, and sees himself partly in the same boat, he certainly does not approve of them, and he is nothing like them himself. In an important sense, they represent what happens when the respectable virtues are rejected outright—the good like duty, justice, responsibility along with the bad—and for Twain the last state is clearly worse than the first.

Huck himself, and to a great extent Jim, are wholly different from this. They represent not the rejection of society's highest values, but their fulfillment. The irony here is that society rejects Huck for being too good; by living up to its own ideals he becomes unfamiliar, and offers a challenge which can easily be mistaken for something stupid, or skeptical, or subversive. On the raft, Huck and Jim become what Lionel Trilling has called a "community of saints"; yet their values come not from the civilized society which is supposed to encourage saints, but from the older incentive of a common danger, a common humanity, a common predicament.

It is here that the most penetrating ironic effects take place. The fact that Huck thinks himself worse, rather than better, than his fellows leads to the major irony that from first to last he sees the help he gives Jim as a sin; and the notion of selling Jim back into bondage can repeatedly present itself as a prompting to repentance and virtue. There are the harrowing moments when he wavers; and the final victory when he says "All right, I'll go to Hell then" is all the more powerful for being unrecognized by Huck himself as savoring of either paradox or irony.

Nor should one underestimate the nature of Huck's stand at this moment. A large part of the country's economy depended on slavery, and one knows for a fact that even tender consciences have difficulty in seeing very clearly when this is so. Again and again the point is underlined. The question is asked, ''Anyone hurt?'' and Huck answers, quite naturally, ''No mum; one nigger killed.'' The doctor towards the end of the tale assumes that recapturing a runaway slave is a more pressing moral duty than attending to a patient. Huck himself is horrified to think that Tom Sawyer might have degenerated into a ''nigger stealer,'' and is relieved to discover that this is not so. All of this may be slightly exaggerated for purposes of the irony, but truth can sometimes defy a satirist to improve upon it for his purpose. The depth to which an economic condition causes moral blindness is deeper, at any rate, than Huck's conscious moralizing can reach. Huck really thinks he *is* being wicked, and the irony here cuts straight from writer to reader, bypassing Huck himself, though enhancing his stature.

One can see, from this central point, what Mark Twain is really doing. Though he rejects ideals that strike him as facile or dangerous, he holds passionately to the conviction that underlies all true radical feeling: namely, that all men should be treated as equally human, irrespective of the natural or man-made barriers of color, class, belief or what you will. That men are not equally good he acknowledges, and that some are too bad to be tolerated he also admits. But that a man should be despised simply for being brought up in poverty, like Huck, or for being the wrong color, like Jim, fills him with outrage. In presenting the pair of them as the salt of the earth he is making a most profoundly radical point. He is also doing more. The decency of Huck and Jim offers some hope for the human species itself: an original virtue, perhaps, constantly departed from, and paradoxically exiled, yet ultimately not to be eradicated from the human heart.

The episode I now want to consider is the very famous one, felt by many readers to be the high point of the novel's greatness. Huck, having been separated from Jim in a fog, and been mourned by him as dead, returns, and plays a joke of Tom Sawyer's kind. (It is very similar, in fact, to the one played by Tom Sawyer on Aunt Polly in the earlier book.) Jim's honest joy at seeing him again he puts down to drink: he hasn't been away, he says, Jim must have imagined it all. So great is Jim's trust in Huck, that he sits thinking for five minutes, and then decides to believe Huck before the evidence of his own senses. ''Well, den, I reck'n I did dream it, Huck; but dog my cats ef it ain't de powerfullest dream I ever see.'' Huck allows Jim to give an account of the "dream," together with an ingenious interpretation, and at the end, by pointing out certain things which do not fit in, makes Jim realize that he has been fooled. The episode continues as follows.

> Jim looked at the trash, and then looked at me, and back at the trash again. He had got the dream fixed so strong in his head that he couldn't seem to shake it loose and get the facts back into its place again, right away. But when he did get the thing straightened around, he looked at me steady, without ever smiling, and says:
>
> "What do dey stan' for? I's gwyne to tell you. When I got all wore out wid work, en wid de callin' for you, en went to sleep, my heart wuz mos' broke bekase you wuz los', en I didn' k'yer no mo' what become er me en de raf'. En when I wake up en fine you back agin', all safe en soun', de tears come en I could a got down on my knees en kiss' yo' foot I's so thankful! En all you wuz thinkin' 'bout wuz how you could make a fool uv ole Jim wid a lie. Dat truck dah is *trash;* en trash is what people is dat puts dirt on de head er dey fren's en makes 'em ashamed."
>
> Then he got up slow, and walked to the wigwam, and went in there, without saying anything but that. But that was enough. It made me feel so mean I could almost kissed *his* foot to get him to take it back.
>
> It was fifteen minutes before I could work myself up to go and humble myself to a nigger—but I done it, and I warn't sorry for it afterwards, neither. I didn't do him no more mean tricks, and I wouldn't done that one if I'd a knowed it would make him feel that way.

Almost any comment on this is bound to be clumsy; it is one of the most memorable moments in literature. In Tom Sawyer's world, a joke of this type would be more or less in order; personal relationships matter less, affections, emotions, sensibility are all blunted or suppressed to the necessary degree. Here, on the raft, it is supremely wrong, as Huck comes to *feel,* as usual without entirely understanding why. In fact, the lies he has told Jim are not his type of lies, and his moral imagination has for once let him down. The law of the raft has been broken, and personal affection sacrificed to a cheap, though not malicious, victory on points. The behavior of Huck and Jim at this moment, free as it is of the sentimentality or the embarrassment which normally surrounds and inhibits such feelings, is both moving and authentic. The values of the raft here reach a moment of undeniable and unforgettable reality.

IV

Mark Twain's irony, I have insisted, is a direct communication between the writer and reader. No one at all in the novel, including

Huck, knows that the raft is a place of virtue; it is the secret communication of the irony. Mark Twain's greatness as a writer can be demonstrated from the skill with which he uses Huck's obtuseness about his own worth as part of his own technique, yet enhances rather than damages him as a person in so doing. It can also be shown from the lack of any arbitrary traps in his work of the Swiftian kind. The reader is challenged wholly at the level of moral response; failure to perceive the direction of the irony is indistinguishable from failure to perceive Huck's virtue. The irony is, indeed, a forcing into the consciousness of readers more educated than Huck himself the reality, as he embodies them, of their own ideals.

The end of the novel, I have contended, is the final insight that Twain has to offer, the final twist of his technique towards truth. It is right, psychologically and historically as well as structurally, that Tom Sawyer should come into the ascendant again; he is, after all, a leader, and Huck and Jim will naturally start trusting him again more than they trust themselves. We can be sure, however, that whatever happens to Huck, as the long process of "civilizing" him starts afresh, he will be a good man. The values which Twain's irony have been establishing will stand more chance of survival because he is in the world, even though they will never have an unambiguous victory. There will be a redemptive possibility at the heart of what Mark Twain elsewhere calls the "damned human race," underlying the cruelty, the muddle and the squalor. Naïve cynicism, like naïve idealism, will not after all have the last word.

For the rest? Goodness might not have a sure triumph, Mark Twain seems to imply, but it has some claim on the universe nonetheless. Huck's enjoyment of life, his honesty, his reverence and charity deserve to be respected; whatever happens he will somehow be all right, as Jim says when telling his fortune. The claim might be solely by way of our own human moral sense; the Mississippi itself will flow on, caring little who worships and enjoys it and who does not. Yet Huck and Jim, with whatever indifference the river might return their worship, remain undefeated, and one feels it is right that they should. This, too, is part of Mark Twain's feeling for life; a reason why Hemingway is wrong to say he cheats at the end, why Dr. Leavis, Lionel Trilling and others are right to find him one of the great writers of moral health.

Bruce King

Huckleberry Finn

Each nation has its own ideals of conduct. Huckleberry Finn is an example of the American hero who, unhampered by any prejudice, experiences life fully, and lives by a personal code of conduct, without reference to the judgments of society. While the code is undefined, its main characteristics are the primacy of personal moral judgments, a belief in the equality of man, and a distrust of society as erecting barriers against, or corrupting, the free movement of the spirit. This absolute internationalization of moral values is peculiarly American. It is just the opposite of the paradigm offered by Jane Austen in *Mansfield Park,* where religion governs morals, morals govern conduct, and conduct governs manners, with the result that a person's spiritual worth may be assessed from his habits and social behavior. It is also unlike the determinism found in the novels of George Eliot or Thomas Hardy.

Huckleberry Finn is a spiritual autobiography. Its main themes are the development of Huck's acceptance of Jim as an equal:

> It was fifteen minutes before I could work myself up to go and humble myself to a nigger—but I done it, and I warn't ever sorry for it afterwards, neither. I didn't do him no more mean tricks, and I wouldn't done that one if I'd a knowed it would make him feel that way.

and his willingness to be rejected by society and risk damnation so that Jim may escape:

> And then think of *me!* It would get all around, that Huck Finn helped a nigger to get his freedom; and if I was to ever see anybody from that town again, I'd be ready to get down and lick his boots for shame. . . .

Reprinted with permission from Ariel, *II (October, 1971), 69–77. Copyright* © *1971,* Ariel: A Review of International English Literature.

"All right, then, I'll *go* to hell"—and tore it up.

It was awful thoughts, and awful words, but they was said. And I let them stay said; and never thought no more about reforming. I shoved the whole thing out of my head; and said I would take up wickedness again, which was in my line, being brung up to it, and the other warn't. And for a starter, I would go to work and steal Jim out of slavery again.

The *persona* of Huckleberry Finn, with its seeming naiveté and implied ironies at the expense of those supposedly more sophisticated or educated, has its roots in regional American folk humor. The uniqueness of the novel results from the bringing together of spiritual autobiography with the comic strategies of the American tall tale. It is this combination, with the folk element setting the tone, which creates the main character and narrator of the story whose words structure our response.

The importance of the journey in *Huckleberry Finn* is not just the structural support which it provides for the stringing together of events; the journey down the river on the raft is the American equivalent of the journey of moral education found in European literature. The archetype of the journey is the traditional allegory of the soul's pilgrimage through this world. The journey is always an individual task or at best shared with a few companions. Whereas in the European novel the use of an orphan or foundling allows the author to create a character without social roots who can try on identities and experience life to the fullest. *Huckleberry Finn* gives the literary tradition a new direction. Huck travels socially downward, away from Miss Watson to the company of Jim, and away from society to the raft, as a necessary process of his spiritual education.

Civilization, as represented by the Mid-West with its churchgoing, elementary, book-learning and middle-class manners, is shown as restrictive, and against the free play of the spirit: "but it was rough living in the house," "living in a house, and sleeping in a bed pulled on me pretty tight." When Huck sleeps in the woods: "That was a rest to me." In his old clothes he is "free and satisfied." In his new clothes he feels "all cramped up." When the widow rings the bell for supper "you had to come." "You couldn't go right to eating." "Don't put your feet up there, Huckleberry." "Don't scrunch up like that." "Don't gap and stretch." "Why don't you try to behave." "She kept pecking at me, and it got tiresome and lonesome." Huck's father may be cruel and terrifying, but Huck feels more at ease with him in the woods than in civilization: "It was kind of lazy and jolly, laying off comfortable all day, smoking and fishing, and no books nor study. . . . It was pretty good times up in the woods there."

There is a significant parallel between Jim's relation to civilization and Huck's. Both are outcasts, without social roots. Huck "lights out" whenever civilization becomes too confining. Jim "lit out" as soon as he suspects he is to be sold down the river. Huck's wish to be free of any entanglements is paralleled by Jim's: "I owns myself." Slavery is the main symbol of the relation of the individual to society, slavery being an undeniable instance of restraint in contrast to natural freedom.

Civilization in *Huckleberry Finn* seems to prevent any spontaneous love of others. Class, money, race and decorum inhibit or corrupt natural feelings. The lack of charity towards others found in civilization (in contrast to the tolerance Jim and Huck feel towards almost everyone) is illustrated by slavery and the selling of human beings. This motif occurs in various transformations during the novel. Miss Watson considers selling Jim down the river, and Tom plays tricks on him. When Tom has used Jim for his adventures at Aunt Sally's he "give Jim forty dollars for being prisoner for us so patient." The king and the duke offer a parallel to such attitudes by selling the Wilks's slaves and betraying Jim. Civilization seems to consist of cruelties perpetrated upon others, whether to inculcate manners, to establish one's dignity, for financial gain, or simply from malice. The Grangerfords and Shepherdsons kill in cold blood. The cruel treatment of animals by the loafers in Arkansas reveals a similar callousness at a lower level of society. Their idea of fun is "putting turpentine on a stray dog and setting fire to him, or tying a tin pan to his tail and see him run himself to death." Sherburn's shooting of Boggs and the attempt to lynch Sherburn are both aspects of the same society. (Jim, if he had been caught, would have been lynched the night Huck disappeared.)

The contrast between conventional pieties and Huck's innate, untutored moral sense is Twain's central irony:

> I went and told the widow about it, and she said the thing a body could get by praying for it was "spiritual gifts." This was too many for me, but she told me what she meant—I must help other people, and do everything I could do for other people, and look out for them all the time, and never think about myself. This was including Miss Watson, as I took it. I went out in the woods and turned it over in my mind a long time, but I couldn't see no advantage about it—except for the other people—so at last I reckoned I wouldn't worry about it any more, but just let it go. . . .
>
> . . . And when she got through, they all jest laid theirselves out to make me feel at home and know I was amongst friends. I felt so ornery and low down and mean, that I says to myself, My mind's made up; I'll hive that money for them or bust.

Compare Huck's reaction to the tar and feathering of the king and duke,

I was sorry for them poor pitiful rascals, it seemed like I couldn't ever feel any hardness against them any more in the world. It was a dreadful thing to see. Human beings *can* be awful cruel to one another.

with

> "Good gracious! Anybody hurt?"
> "No'm. Killed a nigger."
> "Well, it's lucky; because sometimes people do get hurt."

The spontaneous concern for others, without hope of reward, is, it seems, only found in those outside society, such as Huck and Jim. Jim would rather be caught than not send for a doctor to help Tom. The doctor, however, is less concerned with his patients than with keeping Jim captive:

> I had a couple of patients with the chills, and of course I'd of liked to run up to town and see them, but I dasn't, because the nigger might get away, and then I'd be to blame.

There is a difference between *Huckleberry Finn* and most English or European novels of spiritual growth. In European novels the young boy would mature and eventually take his place in society. He would become wiser, be converted, assimilated, initiated, and develop from adolescence to manhood. Huck does not grow up. He is not assimilated into society, nor does he find his spiritual fulfillment in a church, ideology or woman. He remains isolated and alone, young, longing to go West. Bringing standards of the European novel to *Huckleberry Finn* would require us to say that the lack of resolution shows the immaturity of Twain's vision, since he cannot imagine a future for Huck. But the European novel has its own standards, according to which man belongs in society and must find his place, although the place may not at first be apparent. Twain's vision is more pessimistic. There is no place in society for Huck. He must reject society if he is to avoid the infringements upon the spirit found in those who are "civilized." There is no society where Huck will be left in peace with his moral innocence, natural spiritual gifts, and his lack of concern for the status which goes with cultural acquisitions.

When Huck speaks of going West at the end of the novel, it is a rejection of the encroachment of Europe into the American heartland. In terms of American cultural history it represents the desire to find in the West a new Eden, a state of innocence which the pilgrim fathers had sought in the New World. Civilization is the opposite of this. The middle-class respectability of Aunt Sally from which Huck flees is the serpent in the garden. It is the temptation to rebuild Europe in the New World.

The implied criticism of Europe exists upon various levels. The most obvious satire is the many barbs directed at Sir Walter Scott's romances. It would be a mistake to see this as merely an attack on another literary tradition. It is European culture as represented by Scott which is Twain's target. Tom Sawyer, carried away by historical romances, keeps planning escapades which have no basis in reality:

> We used to hop out of the woods and go charging down on hogdrovers and women in carts taking garden stuff to market, but we never hived any of them. Tom Sawyer called the hogs "ingots," and he called the turnips and stuff "julery" and he would go to the cave and pow-wow over what we had done and how many people we had killed and marked. But I couldn't see no profit in it.

Tom's sensibility has been so influenced by a romantic view of European history that he can speak of murder and kidnapping without any awareness of their moral implications.

The indignities to which Tom subjects Jim have a specific thematic function. Whereas Huck makes a moral decision to risk his body and soul to save Jim, Tom sees Jim's captivity as an excuse for adventures. That Tom knows Jim has been set free does not justify his callousness at the expense of Jim's health and feelings. The difference between Huck and Tom is not merely between two personalities; it is between two ethics, two ways of life. Huck, traveling without any cultural baggage, embodies the Puritan ethic as it is found in the New World, with its sense of isolation, desire for self-sufficiency and emphasis on personal moral choice. European culture, as represented by literature, stimulates Tom's imagination, but breeds no knowledge of what is useful or what is morally right.

It may at first seem surprising that *Huckleberry Finn* includes a conscious rejection of Europe; but if we look at the novel carefully, we see that Europe comes into it very often. The king and duke, with their spurious titles and pretended cultural knowledge, represent what Europe has become in the New World. They present a parallel to the conventional social and religious pieties of Miss Watson and Aunt Sally. The king and duke almost get away with their swindles because of the respect given by provincial Americans to supposed representatives of Europe. Twain is, of course, mocking the provincialism of American society; but the mockery is not directed at those who lack a better knowledge of European civilization. It is directed at the ready acceptance of anything which smacks of culture:

> Uncle Silas he had a noble brass warming-pan which he thought considerable of, because it belonged to one of his ancestors with a long wooden handle that come over from England with William the Conqueror in the *Mayflower* or one of them early ships and was hid away up garret with a lot of other old pots and things that was valuable, not on account of being any account because they warn't, but on account of them being relicts, you know.

Some of the episodes which at first seem unrelated to the main story also offer illustrations of the effect of Europe on America. Colonel Sherburn's cold-blooded killing of Boggs is an example of a feudal code of honor which leads to moral stupidity. Though Sherburn has an undeniable dignity, our response to the shooting is assured by the screams of Bogg's daughter. The Shepherdson-Grangerford feud is another example of European codes of honor continuing in the South. Twain is explicit about this. Colonel Grangeford is a gentleman. "He was well born." The Grangerfords and Shepherdsons are both described as "aristocracy." They are not products of the frontier. An ironic contrast is provided when Jim calls Huck "de on'y white genlman dat ever kep' his promise to ole Jim." Of course not every representative of civilization in *Huckleberry Finn* is corrupt or amoral. Widow Douglas and Aunt Sally are well-intentioned and, as Huck says, they mean no harm.

Just as Twain admired *Don Quixote* for sweeping medieval chivalry out of existence, so Huck's journey is a Quixotic voyage through American cultural landscape, with Jim taking the part of Sancho Panza:

> I told Jim all about what happened inside the wreck, and at the ferryboat; and I said these kinds of things was adventures; but he said he didn't want no more adventures. . . .
>
> "It lays in de way Sollermun was raised. You take a man dat's got on'y one er two chillen; is dat man gwyne to be waseful o' chillen? No, he ain't; he can't 'ford it. *He* knows how to value 'em. But you take a man dat's got 'bout five million chillen runnin' roun' de house, en it's diffunt. *He* as soon chop a chile in two as a cat. Dey's plenty mo'. A chile er two, mo' er less, warn't no consekens to Sollermun, dad fetch him!" . . .
>
> "Well," says he, "dat's all right, den. I doan' mine one er two kings, but dat's enough."

Twain's complete rejection of what has been described above as the European cultural tradition can best be seen in the language of *Huckleberry Finn*. The spelling errors, the regional idioms, the poor grammar and general air of semi-literacy, are not mere cleverness. The impersonation of Huck may be a *tour de force* of style, showing the possibilities of a realistic use of the American language, but it also involves a conscious rejection of imitation English writing. To come to *Huckleberry Finn* after reading earlier American literature is like being relieved of a burden, a burden of fine writing, swollen cadences, circumlocutions, long sentences, a certain pomposity. The burden is English prose of the previous two and a half centuries. It is the same burden which was willingly carried by Henry James and rejected by Hemingway. The difference is between a style which attempts to place man in society and make minute observations on such relationships, and a style which reveals what is capable of articulation in those who feel instinctively alienated from the processes and values of society. *Huckleberry Finn* is not, as are the fictions of Jane Austen and George Eliot and Thomas Hardy, a book which grows from the soil of a rich organic culture, closely observed. One notices its lack of texture in comparison to the English novel. Words appear not to carry weight or imply judgments; observed social relations are few and lacking dimension. There is a texture but it is thin, open, and lighter in tone than that of the English novel. It is a texture recognizable in Hemingway's novels and in American painting, where the European tradition of the master artist has been rejected for the appearance of spontaneity and integrity of the self. The way *Huckleberry Finn* begins, with its bad grammar and mockery of Twain's own fiction, is a conscious affront to standards of decorum and high seriousness, which for Twain are part of the heritage of Europe in America.

With our tolerance for youth and rebellion and with our suspicion of civilization, we find Huck modern and contemporary. But this is to assimilate him too easily, just as tolerance for the unconventional and rebellious has to some extent been assimilated into modern culture as a life style without any understanding of what opting out really means. The school teachers who banned *Huckleberry Finn* from school libraries, and the mothers who felt it was not a fit book for their children were on the right track. They felt the way in which *Huckleberry Finn* is an affront to society, a condemnation of the value of education and social conditioning. They understood, if only half consciously, the affront meant to good upbringing and good behavior by the approval Twain gives Huck and by Twain's choice of language. They were quite right to see the novel as somehow subversive, in some way undermining their own aims and objectives in life and what they wished their children to become. Huckleberry Finn is not Tom Sawyer, he is not an imaginative youth destined for the bourgeoisie. He is a rebel with a cause. The cause is to get out of society as fast and as completely as possible for his own ease of mind. The text is clear: "I got to light out for the Territory ahead of the rest, because Aunt Sally she's going to adopt me and sivilize me and I can't stand it. I been there before."

Twain is not a representative of that populist strain of American culture which idolizes the uneducated and the common man. Huck's father illustrates the degeneration of the frontier tradition into populist attitudes:

> I'll learn people to bring up a boy to put on airs over his own father and let on to be better'n what *he* is. You lemme catch you fooling around that school again, you hear? Your mother couldn't read, and she couldn't write, nuther, before she died. None of the family couldn't, before *they* died. *I* can't; and here you're a-swelling yourself up like this. . . .
>
> They call that a govment that can't sell a free nigger till he's been in the State six months. Here's a govment that calls itself a govment, and let's on to be a govment, and thinks it is a govment, and yet's got to set stock-still for six whole months before it can take ahold of a prowling, thieving, infernal, white-shirted free nigger.

While Twain shares with the populist tradition a distrust of Europe, respectability, culture and breeding, the common man doesn't emerge with any honors in *Hucklebrry Finn*. After Boggs is shot people begin pushing and shoving to see the body: "Say, now, you've looked enough, you fellows; 'taint right and 'taint fair, for you to stay thar all the time, and never give nobody a chance; other folks has their rights as well as you." The louts, layabouts and lynch mobs which inhabit the villages along the Mississippi are morally inferior to those who are respectable and educated. The radical rejection of society in *Huckleberry Finn* does not permit any American equivalent to the nostalgia found in the English novel for an older organic community. Huck, isolated, uncorrupted, true to himself, could never be assimilated into any society.

Frank Baldanza

Connecticut Yankee

The most immediately apparent difference between *The Prince and the Pauper* and *A Connecticut Yankee at King Arthur's Court* of 1889 is in the style. The Yankee's sojourn in sixth-century Britain is related here in a cracklingly profane and richly folksy first-person idiom that is perfectly suited to the Mencken-like diatribe against the age of chivalry. By Clemens' own suggestion, the Yankee foreman from the Hartford Colt Factory is a Robinson Crusoe—set down in a brutal, childlike society rotten with the effects of superstition, ignorance, and absolute government. He quietly sets up newspapers, schools, fire departments, insurance companies, a mint, a patent system, a West Point and a naval academy, telephone and telegraph communication, Protestant churches, and traveling soap missionaries to convert people to bathing. Clemens' Yankee, Hank Morgan, represents the inherent assumptions of late nineteenth-century American businessman's democracy as well as Defoe's eighteenth-century castaway represents the British bourgeois values of that day. And from the beginning, it is the manner of the account which most subtly and effectively conditions the reader.

If the story of Edward VI is melodrama, *A Connecticut Yankee* is, refreshingly enough, a "'novel of ideas,'" and should be considered alongside the efforts of Aldous Huxley in the same genre, or G. B. Shaw in drama. It has even closer affinities with Upton Sinclair or Bellamy (who sends his observer into a future utopia rather than an obsolete past).

The book follows no particular party line (aside from the suggestion that some aspects are meant as a defense of Grover Cleveland's administration); it is rather Clemens' own unique refraction of many of the values of his age and environment. With his superior knowledge and

From Mark Twain: An Introduction and Interpretation, *by Frank Baldanza. New York: Barnes & Noble, 1961. Copyright © 1961 by Barnes & Noble, Inc.*

mechanical skill, the ingenious Hank Morgan immediately builds a reputation as a magician that gives him the title of "The Boss." He reforms a whole nation according to the tastes of the sage of Hannibal and Hartford. Personal comfort is as important to him as literacy or anti-Catholicism; the predominant drift of ideas is toward a benevolent, gadget-infested, bustling active industrial democracy. The closest he approaches to doctrinaire didacticism is in The Boss's impassioned defense of Free Trade to a group of benighted Protectionists in Chapter XXXIII.

Clemens was acquainted with Cervantes, and certainly minor incidents here and there, such as the bewitched drove of pigs, recall *Don Quixote*. But the basic situation is the opposite of that in the Spanish classic, since here the hero is the only sane person in a nation of fools, children, and schemers. It is Malory's *Morte d'Arthur* which really sired this satire. Clemens loved the volume, and read it repeatedly, but at least as much for amusement as for enchantment. Long passages in *A Connecticut Yankee* are devoted to burlesquing the style and ideas of this manual of chivalry. Fred W. Lorch has pointed out the additional possibility that an earlier uncompleted novel on feudalism in Hawaii may have given Clemens some of the ideas used in this novel.

Religion is treated largely in Chapters XXI to XXIII, during the Boss's visit to the Valley of Holiness. In general, Clemens tends to view the Catholic Church as an absolutistic, despotic organization that fosters ignorance and superstition and that participates at the side of the nobles in pillaging the helpless masses. W. E. H. Lecky certainly parallels him in some of these attitudes.

Indeed, Clemens informs us that many of the details of Morgan's sojourn in the Valley of Holiness are drawn from Lecky's denunciation of asceticism. The performance centers on the early desert monks to the exclusion of any other evidence. Lecky describes the bowing in prayer of St. Stylite on his pillar; the practical Hank Morgan attaches a power take-off to the saint, and uses his movement as power to run sewing machines to produce shirts. Clemens' clownish prejudice is indicated by his preoccupation with hoary jokes like the Bishop's desiring the *droit du seigneur,* or the monastery on one hill, the convent on the other, and a foundling hospital between the two. In this particular narration, a fountain in the Valley has failed soon after the monks bathed, leading them to suppose that baths are sinful. After Merlin the magician ignominiously fails to restore the spring, the Yankee succeeds spectacularly by plugging up a leak in the well, to the accompaniment of an impressive display of Greek fire, rockets, and roman candles.

The political doctrines of The Boss consist of a wholehearted de-

fense of democracy on the standard American pattern of his day-
—universal male suffrage and separation of church and state. At the
lowest level, it is simply a matter of sermonizing and bald statement:
"any Established Church is an established crime, an established slave-
pen," or "where every man in a State has a vote, brutal laws are
impossible." He excoriates royalty, nobility, and aristocracy in haran-
gues that make up in vituperation for what they lack in support, reasoning, or objectivity. In liberating what King Arthur's culture facetiously
calls "freemen," The Boss specifically abjures revolution on the pattern of Jack Cade or Wat Tyler on the grounds of inefficiency-
—education is the prerequisite to revolution, he says. His answer is to
set up a "Man Factory" for the production of Lecky's kind of Protestant.

Midway in the volume, in Chapters XXVII to XXXVIII, Clemens
resorts to the "schizophrenic" change of identity device he employed in
The Prince and the Pauper when King Arthur voluntarily disguises
himself as a yeoman and travels incognito among his subjects. Clemens
runs through his familiar comic tricks on problems of identity. The Boss
has no end of difficulty at first in training the king to stoop his shoulders, look to the ground, and show the manifold traits of oppression.
Although The Boss is properly horrified by the injustice, cruelty, and
backwardness they encounter, it is not until they are both sold as slaves
that King Arthur vows to abolish at least that social crime from his
realm. Clemens descends periodically to the kind of meretriciously
bathetic sentimentality that mars the story of Tom and Edward. Particularly in such scenes as the burning of a woman at the stake during a
snow storm in order to keep a band of slaves from perishing of cold, and
the hanging of a nursing mother for petty theft, Clemens might have hit
the apogee of late nineteenth-century popular art, but it is embarrassing
to read today. Luckily such scenes do not dominate the volume, although in his treatment of the incredible cruelties of Morgan le Fay, one
almost suspects Clemens of parodying himself.

The same problem arises where melodrama is concerned. Certainly
it dominates the imbroglio in London whereby, after a misfired revolt,
the slaves are to be hanged. They are saved only at the last minute,
when the noose is already around Arthur's neck, by Lancelot and a
troop of knights who arrive on bicycle. Plausibility is stretched so far,
and Clemens' execution is so slipshod, that one is tempted to see this
whole episode, too, as a satiric attack on melodrama. But the explanation is too subtle. As we shall see in the parody attacks on sentimentality
in the Grangerford episodes of *Huckleberry Finn,* Clemens is incapable
of such fine discriminations. His idea of a comic method is like the

well-known advice of the Irishman on the use of the shillelagh, "When you see a head hit it." In a sense, the melodrama here is too preposterously managed even to be taken as satire. Besides, in the aesthetic economy of his day, sentimentality is an inherent part of the melodrama and it is impossible that he meant us to take the sentimental portions of the story seriously and the melodramatic portions lightly.

The climax on the scaffold in Chapter XXXVIII is capped by The Boss's defeating the flower of English chivalry in a joust by using his cowboy lasso and revolvers. Then the book takes another turn in the last five chapters. Morgan is tricked into a long voyage, supposedly for his daughter's health, during which England is torn by internecine feudal warfare, followed by an Interdict imposed by the Church. A pitched battle ensues between The Boss, his trusty aide Clarence, and fifty-four hand-picked boys against the rest of the nation. Blowing up all his factories, schools, and remaining civilized improvements in self-defense, Hank Morgan, isolated on an artificially created island, grimly dynamites and electrocutes 25,000 knights, whereupon all his camp die of the resultant poisoned air. The brutal extravagance of the night scenes in which troop after troop of knights are silently impaled on the electric fences, comes as a distinct surprise. However wide the range of aesthetic effects earlier in the book, there was nothing to prepare the reader for this grim horror. Even though Clemens was deeply concerned, perhaps by now disgusted, with the continuing expenses of the Paige typesetter the dynamite ending does not suggest a repudiation of an industrial economy; it is the first of Clemens' major blasts at the "damned human race." The invincible stupidity and viciousness of the medieval English, even in the face of Hank Morgan's wholesale reforms, necessitates the complete destruction of his new civilization. The people are not worthy of the system.

In the postscript, Twain himself in the nineteenth century witnesses the pathetic death of Morgan who now wishes he were back in the sixth century with his wife and child. Like many another of his books, this is a fantastic hodgepodge; one agrees easily with A. B. Paine that "As an example of Mark Twain at his literary worst and best the *Yankeee* ranks supreme."

Although illustrations in the first editions of all of Clemens' works are interesting and usually of high quality, Dan Beard's work for this volume surpasses most of the other efforts. The pictures reproduce the tone of violent burlesque and buffoonery, frequently with allegorical overtones. In a copy in the J. K. Lilly collection at the Indiana University Library, Beard has identified his models in the margins. The Boss is drawn from a young photoengraver who worked next door to Beard's studio; Clarence is patterned after Sarah Bernhardt; Merlin is Alfred Lord Tennyson; King Arthur is the Kaiser; and the slave driver is Jay Gould!

A Connecticut Yankee was composed over a period of several years, beset by many interruptions and distractions. Clemens wrote portions of it at the home of his friend Twichell, to the accompaniment of loud noises from children at play and carpenters remodeling the house. As noted above, it was written during a period of severe financial strain, when the Paige typesetter was devouring money ravenously; at times, Clemens vowed to race through the book so that he would finish it at the same time the typesetter was completed. But perhaps the most salient influence on the composition was Clemens' burning rages against Matthew Arnold for criticizing General Grant's grammar and America.[1]

In addition, there were difficulties with the British publisher, who was chary about printing the work, and with the critics, who attacked it viciously in some instances. Clemens was hurt and annoyed at this response, and wrote to Andrew Lang to request that his friend do something to right his reputation. His letter . . . is a classically simple apologia that is perhaps the best possible defense of his work as a whole. Lang, however, could not bring himself to praise the *Yankee,* and in his article on Clemens lavished praise where it belongs, on *Huckleberry Finn.*

[1]One is reminded here of Matthew Arnold's classic remarks to Mrs. Howells when he heard that her husband was collaborating with Mark Twain on a comic play: "Oh, but he doesn't like *that* sort of thing, does he?" Paine, *Biography,* p. 758.

Arlin Turner

Mark Twain and the South: Pudd'nhead Wilson

Huckleberry Finn paints the world of the lower Mississippi as the whites see it. To be sure, Huck's level of social vision is little above Jim's, but his sympathy for Jim is inconstant and may seem to imply an identification which does not exist. The white man's doctrine of race superiority is held up to ridicule, but the victim of that doctrine remains unrealized. The basic situation, Huck and Jim raft-borne in flight before expected pursuers, led Mark Twain to formulate in this book a sequence of responses to the arguments on slavery and race he had known since childhood but had never before considered seriously. And even here the reader may get the impression that the sequence grew unawares to the author, while his attention was fixed on other elements.

But Mark Twain had long known that not every slave could expect to go rafting down the river to freedom; recollections extending back to his childhood furnished harsh proof to the contrary. He also knew that the doctrines of race which outlived slavery had far greater effects than to form queer ideas in the mind of a boy such as Huck. In 1874 he had published "A True Story," a short narrative telling that he once asked a Negro servant how she could have lived sixty years and "never had any trouble." She answered by recounting how in slave times her husband and seven children were sold away from her and how she met one son by accident during the Civil War. She concluded, "Oh, no, Misto C————, *I* hain't had no trouble. An' no *joy!*" She thus places herself alongside Jim, a Negro employed to pass judgment on the white man's generalized view of race. But the story, in addition, hints that under suitable prompting the author might trace out the human effects of slavery and caste, and might draw full-scale characters in the process.

Reprinted with permission of the author from "Mark Twain and the South: An Affair of Love and Anger," by Arlin Turner. The Southern Review, IV, n.s. (April, 1968), 493–519. Copyright ©, Arlin Turner.

This hint which may be read in "A True Story" was in a large measure borne out in *Pudd'nhead Wilson,* and the direct promptings under which the novel grew are fully revealed. The author declared that the Negro characters were not in his original plan, and that after he had brought them in for minor roles in the plot, the question of race demanded a hearing without regard to his intentions. When the novel was finished, after extensive recasting, he had treated the dominant Southern issue of his time with more force and realism than elsewhere in his writings—or, for that matter, in any other contemporary writings except Cable's. Here, in a frankness not usual with him, he faced the implications of miscegenation and the psychological effects of racial doctrines on both races. Here, as a consequence, in Roxy, who has one-sixteenth Negro blood, he created his most fully realized female character and through her, in the clearest instance in all his fiction, acknowledged sex to be an element in human relations. As a further consequence, and in spite of inconsistency in the portrait, he achieved in Roxy a level of tragic characterization not present elsewhere in his works. In *Huckleberry Finn* slavery is obscured in the happy ending for Jim, and other aspects of the race question are not broached; *Pudd'nhead Wilson* ends tragically for all the characters, white and black, who are touched by slavery and race.

The author's plans for *Pudd'nhead Wilson* changed radically as the writing progressed. His assertion that the characters, chiefly Roxy, took over and directed the story has been taken with the caution such remarks of his normally require. In this instance, however, two preserved manuscripts make it possible to trace out in detail the growth of the book, and they show his statements about the composition to be mainly true—in essence if not in literal fact. Studying his habits in numbering pages and making additions and deletions has been rewarding. Cancelled numbers on some of the pages, to cite one aspect of the evidence, show that those pages occupied three positions before being placed finally.

Pudd'nhead Wilson recounts what follows after Roxy exchanges two babies in their cradles: her son, a thirty-second part Negro, and the son in an aristocratic white family. Her son, growing up as the white Tom Driscoll, abuses Chambers, the other changeling; he becomes dissolute, turns to robbery, and finally kills Judge Driscoll, his supposed uncle, in a robbery attempt. The title character uses fingerprints to convict Tom of the murder. Several auxiliary characters, including Italian twins, furnish a thread of extravagant comedy. In the original full-length manuscript the twins were conjoined (Siamese) twins, but before the work was published they were separated in what the author called "a literary caesarean operation," and most of the episodes involving them initially were moved to an appended section with the title "Those Extraordinary Twins."

Mark Twain explained that he first planned to write "an extravagant sort of a tale," a "howling farce," about conjoined twins. After he had written ten thousand words, a long sequence of improvising began. He had decided to write a book, not a brief story; he introduced Pudd'nhead Wilson, whose hobby of collecting fingerprints would be the means of apprehending a robber, Tom Driscoll. At this point Roxy is introduced for the first time. She is identified at once as Tom's mother, though only she and Tom know, and soon allows herself to be sold back into slavery, some years after she has been freed, so that he can pay his gambling debts and protect his inheritance. The author had decided to augment the role of Pudd'nhead Wilson by having him identify Tom not only as a robber but also as a Negro. In what he wrote from this point onward, Mark Twain added very little further on the twins; for when Roxy wandered into the story, as he phrased it, she introduced a note of tragedy which he discovered finally to be incompatible with the farce he had first planned. Study of the manuscript reveals that after proceeding to the end of the story, in his revised plan, the author turned back and added more than two hundred pages to fill in the background for the action. The additions, along with the recasting and revising which can be identified on the earlier sheets, show the author moving hesitatingly and erratically toward views which he had not held before on slavery, race superiority, miscegenation, and the effects of race doctrine on the whites. He had never before been led along the steps which now brought him to face these issues directly.

The chief need in recasting the story was to adjust the characters Tom Driscoll and Roxy to the new understanding of the race problem the author was approaching. The roles these two had assumed were leading him to understand that slavery and caste shape not only society and its institutions but individuals also, that instead of being merely a social phenomenon, miscegenation is a matter of life and a matter of death among human beings.

As initially introduced, Tom Driscoll is white, with no hint of Negro blood. He is a young man of both innate and cultivated evil, displaying villainy enough to deserve the conviction for crime Pudd'nhead Wilson's fingerprint collection will insure. He embarrasses his friends when he can, robs his neighbors to finance his dissolute life, and gleefully contemplates killing his uncle if that is necessary to hasten his own inheritance.

Such was the character Tom when the author decided to make him a changeling and a Negro. The Tom of the second stage, accustomed to abusing the slaves as members of an inferior race, is grimly embittered to learn that he belongs to that race. In the first draft of the episode in which Roxy tells him who she is, she refuses to identify his father, leaving him consumed by hatred. Vowing to learn the secret from her somehow and to seek out and kill his father, he exults in what he calls his father's death song. He will show what can be expected from "a nigger with a grievance," repeating the word "nigger" in his bitterness. The lowly creature who is his mother, he says, has a nobility beyond anything a slaveholder could ever claim. He is himself both a slave and a white man's bastard. Whatever is base in him may have come from either the white or the black blood, or from both, for it is the product of slavery, through the abuse and degradation experienced by the slaves or through the debasement and tyranny produced in the slaveholder. Tom's resentment inspires in him a raging hatred of all whites and a dedication to revenge which bear overtones of the heroic. His hatred produces the courage he would not otherwise have, and he is capable of murder, not simply assassination. Notebook entries and preserved manuscript scraps show that Mark Twain at one time planned a scene in which Tom confronts his father, hesitates, and then concludes he cannot kill him. But when his father pleads, "O spare me!—I am your father!" Tom cries, "Now for *that*, you shall die," and kills him.

Because the inordinate deceit and meanness and cowardice of the white Tom Driscoll could have no place in this Tom, the author turned back to pages written earlier and modified these aspects of his character. Yet some traits appropriate to the earlier Tom but not this one remained unchanged, and survived in fact to the printed book, such as Tom's goading of Pudd'nhead Wilson about his hobbies and his failure in law practice.

Mark Twain's uncertainty in delineating Tom as the Negro who had been brought up believing he was white suggests that he was exploring his way in areas new to his thought and that more than once he decided he had gone astray in his extemporizing. This Tom Driscoll of hatred and revenge was not acceptable, even after the diabolism of the earlier white man had been diluted. A character who nursed such blind hatred, however many wrongs he might have suffered, seemed to Mark Twain false to the Negro in America, either as a slave or as a freedman. In further—and final—recasting, therefore, Roxy tells Tom he can hold his head high in pride because his father, who died ten years earlier, belonged to one of the First Families of Virginia. Tom's earlier rage against his unknown father now becomes self-pitying analysis of his own weaknesses and a cowering humility in the presence of whites. He is weak, cowardly, given to drink and gambling, incapable of hunting down and killing his father or anyone else. He kills Judge Driscoll when frightened during a robbery rather than by design.

The changes in character Roxy experiences in the sequences of revisions, no less drastic than the changes in Tom, show even more clearly the expansion that was taking place in the author's understanding of Negro character and Negro experiences in America. At her first appearance in the early draft, sick and penniless and whining as she returns from eight years as a chambermaid on the river, Roxy is a stock household Negro, visiting among the servants and living on food they sneak out of the kitchen for her. She has little thought of her son Tom, except that she hopes he will provide for her. Rebuffed in her first pleas to him, she makes a whimpering appeal to his sympathy. Then when she tells Tom who he is and can blackmail him, she becomes a partner in his burglary and frightens him by the risks she will take in her greed. Portions of the early draft show her finally driving Tom, under awesome threats, to steal from Judge Driscoll the money he needs. One manuscript fragment concludes with her saying to Tom: " 'Take yo' choice—hog de money dis night or I tells de Jedge in de mawnin' who you *is*. You'll be on de oction block in 2 minutes.' " Another fragment illustrates Roxy's meanness as she was first drawn. Chambers has been arrested by mistake after Tom's murder of Judge Driscoll. When he has been seized by a lynch mob, Roxy says, "Well twould a ben my son if I hadn't changed 'em."

In the revisions, Roxy's heartlessness and her calculated selfishness are cancelled. She shows genuine affection for Tom when she returns from steamboating, and she is confident he will treat her kindly. When his harshness has convinced her "that her beautiful dream was a fond and foolish vanity, a shabby and pitiful mistake," she has feelings altogether unsuited to the early Roxy: "she was hurt to the heart, and so ashamed that for a moment she did not quite know what to do or how to act." To Tom's continued degrading scorn, she responded as "the heir of two centuries of unatoned insult and outrage," and "the fires of old wrongs flamed up in her breast and began to burn fiercely." Thus the reader of the published work is prepared to have Roxy take on the role of an avenging angel as she tells Tom who he is. Instead of the scheming woman of the earlier draft who would drive her son to destruction for her own gain, she now goes into slavery to save his fortune. He sells her into what they both know to be the unspeakable horror of slavery "down the river," and after her escape and return she is simply pronouncing on him, in effect, the sentence he has brought upon himself—he must go ask the judge for the money to buy her free. To rob the judge rather than ask for the money is now his decision, not Roxy's. It is worth noting that in the early draft Roxy is normally referred to as a mulatto, a crone, or an old woman, and that in the revisions such designations are replaced by her name or a simple pronoun. In one revision it is said that Roxy's "bearing took to itself a dignity and state that might have passed for queenly if her surroundings had been a little more in keeping with it."

Although slavery and race oppression were introduced late into the plans for *Pudd'nhead Wilson*, in the final version they stand under severe and inclusive charges. The helplessness of the slaves is dramatized in Tom's abuse of Chambers, for example; and the catalog of horrors Roxy experiences after she has been re-sold into slavery gains immediacy and weight from the fact that she describes them to her son, who has betrayed her. The effects of slavery on the slaves, aside from their lot of deprivation and pain, appear in Chambers, when at the end he discovers he is white but cannot recover from the wrenching in both mind and spirit he has received while a slave. After learning that he is in fact a Negro and a slave, Tom finds he can no longer think and act as he did before, even though he and Roxy alone know his identity. In addition, the effect of slavery on the master class becomes clear, as Mark Twain exposes the essential dishonesty entailed by the owning of slaves. Percy Driscoll feels so righteous for selling his three household slaves, not down the river but elsewhere, after they have confessed to petty thievery, that he wants the account to serve his son as an example of moral conduct. Tom, growing up the spoiled heir to a Virginia gentleman's estate, develops the cruelty appropriate in that estate to dealings with slaves. His arrogance and his inhumanity as a white man and also his cowardice and meanness later as a slave derive from his own or the experiences of others as slaves or as slaveowners.

The extent to which Roxy led the author to consider subtler aspects of the race question than ever before becomes clear in a comparison of *Pudd'nhead Wilson* with *The American Claimant*, published a year earlier but written concurrently with early drafts of *Pudd'nhead Wilson*. The slaves Uncle Dan'l and his wife Jinny, along with other characters, are derived from *The Gilded Age*, in which they are sold down the river in a bankruptcy sale. After emancipation they come back home faithfully, in *The American Claimant*, and are taken in, even though they are too old to work and in fact must have hired servants to look after them. These characters, originating in two servants the author knew at Hartford in 1875, are stereotyped black clowns, arguing about divine providence and other concepts equally beyond their minds.

It is a long step from Uncle Dan'l and Jinny to Roxy and Tom, but it should be noted that the Negro as a simple comic figure appears also in *Pudd'nhead Wilson*. Jasper, first named Jim in the manuscript, and then Sandy (for a slave in the Clemens household in Hannibal), appears in the second chapter in a bantering dialogue with Roxy. In the initial draft Jasper is a Dunker Baptist and Roxy is a Shouting Methodist, as are also Dan'l and Jinny, and they too argue about divine providence. In marking out the debate of Jasper and Roxy on divine providence, the author reduced the buffoonery of the Negro characters, but the tone of the scene remained slapstick. Mark Twain's fondness for these characters, with their comical argument, is attested further by their appearance again in a work he left unpublished, *Simon Wheeler, Detective* (1963).

Along with the subject of race, Mark Twain looked more closely in *Pudd'nhead Wilson* than elsewhere in his works at the cult of Southern aristocracy, codes of honor, and the duel, as details of the plot led him from one aspect of the cult to another. Yet he reached no consistent, inclusive attitude, and he displayed a tolerance of slavery as seen from the position of the slaveholders which in the total view is out of keeping with the view of slavery shown through the slaves.

In the past he had thrown many darts at the Sir Walter Scott cult in the South: the naming of children, houses, colleges, and towns from Scott's romances; the importing of unfitting medieval architecture; the revival of the tournament; the awe with which Americans viewed titled Europeans; the taste for medieval romances of adventure; and above all the assumption of class superiority. But Mark Twain acknowledges varying types and grades of aristocracy, and he makes no claim that they are confined within the South. Laura Hawkins, in *The Gilded Age*, finds one type in Washington she considers genuine. "The Curious Republic of Gondour" (1875) postulates an aristocracy of weighted ballots intended to eliminate flaws in government, greatest weight going to education, next greatest to property. Sally Sellers in *The American Claimant* resides in Kenilworth Keep of Redgauntlet Hall, near Rob Roy Hall, at Rowena-Ivanhoe College, where there are "castellated college-buildings—towers and turrets and an imitation moat—and everything about the place named out of Sir Walter Scott's books and redolent of royalty and state and style." She is ready to become Lady Gwendolyn, but later realizes that she is no less silly than her father in his pursuit of an earldom. Brought to wisdom by love, she decides that genuine aristocracy in its proper place is right; at the same time the son of an earl realizes the folly of leaving his inheritance for a humble role in America. The two are married and depart for England to take up his rightful station. European titled aristocracy stands condemned, but only mildly. The severest strictures are against American pretensions to aristocracy, and much of American life stands indicted through the idealism of the young English nobleman. But his idealism is folly, after all. One man cannot reform an entire social order alone; the sensible course for him is to keep his hereditary station and work for improvement from that as a base.

In *Pudd'nhead Wilson* the First Families of Virginia are represented by Percy Northumberland Driscoll, York Leicester Driscoll, Pembroke Howard, and Tom's father, Colonel Cecil Burleigh Essex. These men, bearing flamboyantly appropriate names, revere their Virginia heritage above all other affiliations, not excluding the loyalties owed to church, state, or family. In this loyalty they are foolish rather than evil, and they possess the virtues of integrity, kindness, and high purpose. Supported by hereditary doctrines of caste, they are unquestioning slaveholders. Kind masters, according to their lights, they would not believe that the slaves suffered under the system or that they were themselves warped through their role as masters. Slavery is under subtler and stronger indictment in the final than in the earlier drafts of the novel. With Roxy becoming more important and the book swinging from farce toward tragedy, greater subtlety was required and greater force in the satire resulted. But the slaveholders do not appear to be responsible for the evils of slavery. Except in the death of Judge Driscoll, they have farcical roles. In the context of the entire plot, Driscoll is destroyed by an agent of the social evil which his proud heritage has fostered, but this larger view is obscured by the surface fact that he falls before Tom's villainy.

Percy Driscoll no doubt owed much of his character and some of his action as a slaveholder to Mark Twain's recollections of his father, and it is probably for this reason that Driscoll is portrayed more absurd than evil and that Tom is left to bear the full curse of slaveholding. Like John Marshall Clemens, Driscoll has come from Virginia, is proud of his gentlemanly heritage, is the soul of generosity toward white men, but applies a different brand of generosity and kindness in dealing with slaves. In an early draft of *Pudd'nhead Wilson* Mark Twain assigned to Judge Driscoll an episode from his father's life. Once journeying south to collect money a friend had long owed him, John Marshall Clemens took along a slave to sell as a way of financing the trip, thoughtless of the sorrow caused the slave and his family. The cutting out of this journey even before the final revision of the novel was probably due in part to the author's reluctance to perpetuate an episode which reflected so unfavorably on his father. In a similar instance, Mark Twain referred in the manuscript of *Following the Equator* (1897) to his father's striking a slave. When his wife objected, he deleted the note.

A key to the author's uncertain way of looking at the cult of Southern aristocracy may be taken from his equivocation in handling the duel. His account of how once in Nevada he came close to engaging in a duel should be noted in this connection. In a passage deleted from the manuscript of *Life on the Mississippi* he remarked that the duel had not quite disappeared in the Southern states but had been "hopefully modified." In New Orleans blood might be drawn now and then, but in

Virginia, he added, "the mere flash and smell of powder cure the most acrid wound which can be inflicted upon a statesman's honor." The implication here is that duels are to be condemned, but the direct statement—and the cause for scorn—is that in both New Orleans and Virginia dueling is no more than ritual and pretense, with no real danger to the participants. The same statement and the same scorn dominate two chapters in *A Tramp Abroad*. In one the French political duels are ridiculed as utter sham. Another chapter describes the bloody duels of university students in Germany, detailing the blood, pain, and disfigurement as the serious young Germans hack away at each other. The student duels were genuine, and the author could admire the courage, even though it was displayed in a foolish affair.

The duel recounted in *Pudd'nhead Wilson* as first written, and retained in the supplement, "Those Extraordinary Twins," is broadest farce: one of the conjoined twins has accepted Judge Driscoll's challenge and the other twin is an unwilling close attendant. In the novel proper, with the twins separate, the duel remains farcical—with all those present receiving wounds except the principals—but the episode is less outlandish. Even so, not all is farce. Judge Driscoll and his friend, Pembroke Howard, are shown to be naïve, if not absurd, in their reverence for the code of honor; but they are to be respected for integrity and courage lying beyond all question. In pouring her blistering scorn upon Tom because he has refused to defend his honor in a duel, Roxy in effect condemns rather than defends dueling, for like Huckleberry Finn, she speaks from the false beliefs of the society around her. Yet, the reader notes that Tom refuses to fight not because of any principle but because of his cowardice, and his refusal elicits the derision of Pudd'nhead Wilson, who stands outside the social structure of Dawson's Landing and thus speaks from an uncompromised position.

Dueling on Mark Twain's pages is a silly vestige of an antiquated code which was just as silly when it flourished in remote ages. Still, no one loses more than a drop or two of blood in his version of a Southern duel and no one but a cowardly Tom Driscoll or an other-worldly Italian twin refuses to fight. Like feuds duels are total nonsense, but they are perpetuated by families who bear the best blood and the highest culture of the region. The doctrines supporting race superiority and slavery are false growths from man's greed and his habit of deceiving himself; yet the Driscolls, Miss Watson, and other slaveholders of Mark Twain's fictional world seem to be somehow without responsibility for slavery. They are comical or silly or unaware, but always innocent, at least in intentions. Until *Pudd'nhead Wilson* Mark Twain's fictional slaves knew little of actual slavery; and even in that book the typed stage darky is exploited for comic effect. But under prompting from the characters and the situations he introduced into the plot, he reached understandings of the two races and their influences on each other, both before and after emancipation, which he had not approached before.

In 1894, the year *Pudd'nhead Wilson* appeared, George W. Cable published his last book dealing with the race question in the South, *John March, Southerner*. Cable had found no audience in either North or South for essays or lectures on the subject, and his publishers were urging him to write fiction which would not antagonize or even disturb anyone. By 1894, the problems explored in *Pudd'nhead Wilson* had grown wearisome in the North as well as the South. More than a decade earlier the political decision had been made that the Southern states should solve the race problem without interference from the national government. As state laws were enacted in the early 1890s which decreed for the former slaves a segregated, non-voting status, no effective protest was voiced in either section. The public, valuing the peace which had been achieved, did not welcome disturbances, even in fiction.

There is something of irony in that, by chance rather than intention, Mark Twain wrote his most perceptive and most impressive attack on racism and related doctrines at a time when his attack could stir no spark in the reading public. It was an irony fitting to the black mood into which he was descending steadily deeper. Roxy, Tom, Chambers, and Judge Driscoll had revealed to him subtleties in the race question which in his chuckle-headedness, he might have said, he had not learned from Uncle Dan'l, Aunt Hannah, Jim, or others of the characters he had put into fiction over the preceding twenty years. And his new understanding came at just the time he realized—or might have learned from his friend Cable—that society, in the North no less than in the South, had settled into a pattern of thought which could promise no relief for the victims of race oppression.

Whether Mark Twain was aware that these changes were taking place in the status and the prospects of the former slaves, is not certain—or indeed whether he realized that in *Pudd'nhead Wilson* he had probed more deeply than ever before into the complexities of Southern society. He did not attempt in any of his later works to reconcile the inconsistencies and contradictions which remained in that novel—and in his mind—even after the extensive reworking which accompanied refinements in his understanding. He continued, rather, to speak of the South after his old habit, in affection or disgust, nostalgia or anger, depending on the immediate provocation and his mood at the moment.

John R. May

The Gospel According to Philip Traum: Structural Unity in "The Mysterious Stranger"

The major problem with the criticism of "The Mysterious Stranger" to date is that it has been too narrowly concerned with a thematic justification of the last chapter in relation to the rest of the work. The story was unfinished at the time of Twain's death; and it was not until his literary executor, Albert Bigelow Paine, "discovered" the final chapter that the story was eventually published in 1916. Without a final chapter the story undoubtedly lacks a sense of direction, yet critics have had trouble justifying the relationship between the unambiguous solipsism of the last chapter and the earlier development of the story. Is there any preparation in the story for the utter negation of external reality that Philip Traum's revelation in the last chapter represents?

In *Mark Twain and Little Satan,* published in 1963, John S. Tuckey establishes conclusively the order of Twain's composition of the three distinct versions of the Satan story, that Bernard DeVoto had previously named—the Eseldorf Version, the edited text that was actually published; the Hannibal Version, describing the influence of a young Satan named "44" on Tom Sawyer and Huck Finn; and the Print Shop Version, concerned again with "44," but as the dream self of August Feldner. One of Tuckey's conclusions is that Paine's last chapter is actually the conclusion of the Print Shop Version; but since the Eseldorf text was clearly the most developed manuscript, he made the necessary editorial changes so that the Print Shop conclusion would fit the Eseldorf story.[1] His thesis seems to have had little impact on the

---

[1]John S. Tuckey, *Mark Twain and Little Satan* (West Lafayette, Ind.: Purdue University Press, 1963).

Reprinted with permission from Studies in Short Fiction, *VIII (Summer, 1971), 411–422. Copyright © 1971,* Studies in Short Fiction.

present state of criticism of the novel; there is obvious need, therefore, for serious critical study of the manuscripts. The publication of *Mark Twain's Mysterious Stranger Manuscripts* (University of California, 1969), edited by William M. Gibson, will no doubt aid this process. The volume contains the three fragmentary versions, with notes concerning the appearance of the manuscripts and all emendations, cancellations, marginalia—and in whose handwriting. As interesting and informative as these textual investigations will be, though, perhaps criticism will in the final analysis simply have to accept Paine's 1916 version as a kind of literary "fortunate fall"—a masterful piece of editing and, because of its extraordinary power, a work of art in its own right.

The most satisfactory attempts to discover unity in the present manuscript have concentrated on the relationship between the first ten chapters and the conclusion; and since the conclusion is so openly didactic and philosophical, these studies have focused on the thematic development in the earlier chapters. Edwin Fussell finds a coherent development in the story to its solipsistic conclusion; it represents, he says, an objectification of the mental process whereby Theodor discards his mistaken belief in the reality of the world for an acceptance of the reality of dreams alone.[2] (His essay, published ten years before Tuckey's rejection of the last chapter, justifies the acceptance of the Paine conclusion on the grounds that Twain did after all write the chapter; whether he liked it or not, says Fussell, is beside the point.) Pascal Covici thinks that "the most salient feature of *The Mysterious Stranger* is that Theodor's point of view changes and changes radically."[3] William C. Spengemann, seeing this last major work of Twain's in relation to *Tom Sawyer* and *Huckleberry Finn*, believes that the final chapter can be taken as the "logical conclusion" of the events which precede it if it is interpreted in terms of "escape from life in cosmic innocence."[4]

The excellence of these studies is nonetheless marred by the fact that the excessive concern for justifying the final chapter has forced them to be selective. They concentrate on the thematic development of the novella and thereby ignore much of the richness and coherence of the narrative structure. It is hard to see, for example, how their conclusions concerning the thematic unity of the story answer the objections

[2]Edwin S. Fussell, "The Structural Problem of *The Mysterious Stranger*," *Studies in Philology*, XLIX (1952), 95–104.

[3]Pascal Covici, Jr., *Mark Twain's Humor* (Dallas: Southern Methodist University Press, 1962), p. 227.

[4]William C. Spengemann, *Mark Twain and the Backwoods Angel* (Kent, Ohio: Kent State University Press, 1966), p. 127.

raised by Edmund Reiss. "Although beginning auspiciously," he writes, "the novelette tends to become disjointed. The questions of the worth of man, of the ambiguity of good and evil, of the Moral Sense, begin to fade into the background as Twain emphasizes the adventurous part of the story. . . . Incidents that are interesting but distracting begin to appear. In not contributing much to the whole work, many of Theodor's adventures . . . are . . . satirical, curious, but yet, as they stand, not really necessary. It is with the final chapter that 'The Mysterious Stranger' regains the intensity of its opening episodes."[5]

Any satisfactory treatment of the unity of the story will, therefore, have to go beyond the thematic development to show, if possible, how the whole narrative contributes to the development of the discerned underlying theme. It is with this purpose in mind that I offer the following observations concerning the structural unity of "The Mysterious Stranger."

Coleman O. Parsons is credited with making the connection between the portrayal of Satan and the Jesus of the New Testament Apocrypha; there are clear references in Mark Twain's notebook to the impression that the discovery of the Apocryphal Gospels made upon him.[6] His indebtedness to the New Testament, however, whether conscious or unconscious, goes beyond the similarity of characterization. For if there is any principle of structural unity in "The Mysterious Stranger," it is a variation of the Gospel form, which frequently—as in Matthew—juxtaposes the actions and discourses of Jesus within the pattern of his ministry of salvation. In the light of this, "The Mysterious Stranger" becomes a kind of anti-Gospel because the news that it brings is not a celebration of reality but its negation.

The structural unity of "The Mysterious Stranger" develops out of Philip Traum's mission of salvation to Theodor Fischer. The narrative context of this educational process is circumscribed by Traum's three attempts to help Fr. Peter and his household—first, by giving Fr. Peter money to pay his debts; then, by helping Ursula and Marget while Fr. Peter is in jail; and finally, by possessing Wilhelm Meidling during his defense of Fr. Peter at the trial. A moral lesson, presented in the form of a discourse, is drawn from the circumstances surrounding each of these actions—which is rendered universal for Theodor's instruction by Traum's manipulation of time and space. One can demonstrate that all of the narrative lies within this threefold framework, either as descriptive preparation for or dramatic consequence of the action taken, or as

[5]Edmund Reiss, "Foreword" in Mark Twain, *The Mysterious Stranger and Other Stories* (New York: New American Library, 1962). pp. xxiii–xxiv.

[6]Coleman O. Parsons, "The Background of *The Mysterious Stranger,*" *American Literature,* XXXII (1960), 55–74.

illustrative of Satan's discourses. For the purpose of describing the three
segments of the story, it seems advisable to consider the whole novel,
first, on the level of action and discourse, and only then to treat the
significance of the threefold excursion into time and space.

The narrative is set in a dreamy Austrian village in 1590. Austria
itself was asleep, we are told; and Eseldorf "was in the middle of that
sleep, being in the middle of Austria. . . . It was still the Middle Ages
in Austria, and promised to remain so forever."[7] The medieval atmosphere of the village is accentuated as the narrator describes successively
the castle, the absent prince, the importance of Christian training, the
two priests, the astrologer, and the "inquisition."

The finely-sketched introduction quickly reveals the situation out
of which the three narrative strands will develop. Fr. Peter has been
charged "with talking around in conversation that God was all goodness
and would find a way to save all of his poor human children" (p. 163).
The astrologer, Fr. Peter's open enemy—and "a very powerful one"
(ibid.)—because he impressed the bishop with his piety, was suspected
of reporting Fr. Peter's statement to the bishop. Despite pleas for mercy
from the priest's niece, Marget, the bishop "suspended Fr. Peter inde-
finitely" (pp. 163-164). For two years Fr. Peter has been without his
flock, and he and his niece are in serious financial difficulty.

The way is prepared for the appearance of a savior. The morning
after a nocturnal encounter with a ghost at the castle, Theodor Fischer
and his inseparable companions, Seppi Wohlmeyer and Nikolaus
Bauman, are talking over the experiences of the previous evening, in
the shade of a nearby woody hilltop, when a youth comes strolling
toward them through the trees. The handsome stranger tries to put the
boys at ease by miraculously providing the fire that they need to be able
to smoke. He says that his name is Satan, even though he is really only
Satan's nephew. When he is trying to conceal his identity, he uses the
name Philip Traum.

Satan quickly commands the attention and interest of the boys by
creating some tiny people whom he later wantonly destroys because
they begin to argue and fight. Satan's powers both charm and frighten
the boys. They are charmed by his creative ingenuity, yet appalled by
his merciless destruction of the people he has created. From a narrative
viewpoint, this passage serves the purpose of establishing his creden-
tials as one who can achieve the miraculous; it also provides the opportunity for Satan to introduce the thesis of his first discourse: that man is
the victim of the moral sense—"a sense whose function is to distinguish
between right and wrong, with liberty to choose which of them he will

[7]Mark Twain, *The Mysterious Stranger and Other Stories* (New York: New American
Library, 1962), p. 161. Subsequent references to this edition are noted in the text.

do." "He is always choosing," Satan insists, "and in nine cases out of ten he prefers the wrong" (p. 193). This thesis will be developed throughout the first phase of the narrative, which is concerned with the events resulting from Satan's gift to Fr. Peter.

Thus, when Fr. Peter recovers his lost wallet in the presence of the boys and finds it filled with money, the boys know immediately the source of the money—even though they cannot tell because Satan will not allow them to reveal his identity. They nevertheless persuade Fr. Peter to keep the money and use it to pay his debts, until the rightful owner can be found.

The people attribute his good fortune "to the the plain hand of Providence" (p. 180). The ironic interplay of reality and belief is humorously suggested when one or two of the citizens say privately that "it looked more like the hand of Satan," and Theodor observes that "really that seemed a surprisingly good guess for ignorant people like that" *(ibid)*. Celebrating Fr. Peter's good fortune, the boys approach him to ask what the moral sense is. Fr. Peter's answer that "it is the one thing that lifts man above the beasts that perish and makes him heir to immortality" leaves the boys "filled but not fatted" (p. 81).

Fr. Peter's prosperity is short-lived though. Accused by the astrologer of stealing his money, Fr. Peter is put in jail; and his niece and the household are again reduced to penury. Concerned about Fr. Peter, Theodor thinks that he would like to see the jail; and he and Satan are there the next moment because Satan reads his thought. A young man accused of heresy is being tortured on a rack, and Theodor calls it "a brutal thing." Satan's response is a further elaboration of the perversity of the moral sense. "No, it was a human thing," he reminds Theodor; "you should not insult brutes by such a misuse of that word. . . . No brute ever does a cruel thing—that is the monopoly of those with the moral sense" (p. 192). As a further illustration of the point, Satan takes Theodor to a French factory "where men and women and little children were toiling in heat and dirt and a fog of dust" (p. 193). Satan explains "It is the Moral Sense which teaches the factory properietors the difference between right and wrong—you perceive the result" (p. 194). The next moment they are back on the streets of Eseldorf and hearing from Seppi about the mysterious disappearance of Hans Oppert, who has not been seen since he "brutally" struck his faithful dog and knocked out one of his eyes. Satan reminds them "that brutes do not act like that, but only men" (p. 195). His lesson concerning the moral sense is ironically heightened by the fact that the dog, despite his beatings, has been trying in vain to direct the villagers to his dying master; but no one pays any attention to the dog, and Hans dies without absolution.

At this point in the narrative, though, the second strand has already been introduced because as soon as Fr. Peter is imprisoned, Satan helps his household again by giving Ursula, Fr. Peter's servant, the Lucky Cat—"whose owner finds four silver groschen in his pocket every morning" (p. 188). This overlapping of narrative strands is no indication of lack of artistic control, but rather a technique of heightened artistic effect parallel to the overlapping statements of the melody in a fugue.

Human nature being what it is, Ursula hires young Gottfried Narr to help around the house—now that there is an abundance of money. The boys wonder, though, about the wisdom of this decision because Gottfried's grandmother has been burned as a witch, and "the witch-terror had risen higher during the past year than it had ever reached in the memory of the oldest villagers" (p. 198). Theodor tells Satan about Gottfried's grandmother and about eleven schoolgirls all of whom the commission had forced to confess to practicing witchcraft. Satan answers by calling a bullock out of a pasture and emphasizing the fact that animals, like angels, do not have the moral sense and therefore "wouldn't drive children mad with hunger and fright and loneliness," nor would they "break the hearts of innocent, poor old women" (p. 200).

Again Providence was "getting all the gratitude" (p. 202) for the temporary well-being of Fr. Peter's household. But Fr. Adolf and the astrologer begin to suspect witchcraft, especially after Gottfried's remark in the presence of the latter that Marget and Ursula were "living on the fat of the land" (p.201). When other means of detecting witchcraft have failed, they decide that they will use the party Marget has announced as an opportunity to discover with certainty the source of the household's abundance. When they see the house filled with delicacies, knowing that no supplies were brought in all week, they are convinced that it is "witchcraft . . . of a new kind—a kind never dreamed of before" (p. 204). Satan intervenes, though, to cast suspicion back on the astrologer and Fr. Adolf. The situation deteriorates when the possessed astrologer performs stunts in the market square beyond his age and powers. So rampant now is the fear of witchcraft that the townspeople are convinced that God has forsaken them.

These events lead directly into Satan's second discourse. Theodor feels that he has to try to reform Satan and begs him "to be more considerate and stop making people unhappy" (p. 210). They are in China at the time, and Satan explains to Theodor that there is nothing that can be done about the happiness quotient in a human's life. "Every man is a suffering-machine and a happiness-machine combined" (p. 211); and either happiness and suffering are equally divided, or suffering predominates. The principal point of this discourse and of the events that follow it by way of illustration through Chapter Eight seems to be that there is so much necessary misery in human life that death comes as a genuine favor to victimized humanity. The determinism that is preached here does not, as some critics have suggested, imply a denial of the freedom that is necessary to make the perversity of man's moral sense deliberate; it is rather a determinism to misery. If there is any lack of freedom, it is not the freedom of moral choice, but rather the freedom to choose happiness over misery. As a corollary to his instruction concerning the mercy of death in the light of human misery, Satan anticipates his ultimate denial of the reality of an afterlife by denying the existence of purgatory and implying that there is no heaven.

The whole discussion of the inexorable sequence of man's acts —like the toppling of bricks laid in a row—is placed within the context of man's inability to know good fortune from bad because he cannot see into the future, where there is nothing but misery. Man's "first childish act" (p. 215), which situates him in particular circumstances, in a certain environment, can hardly be important from a moral point of view; it is simply the origin of his misery because it is the beginning of a life that only death can happily terminate. Satan, who can see all the possible careers open to an individual, knows that the only favor that can be done for a human being is either to terminate his life or to make him insane. The subsequent events in this second strand illustrate the mercy of death; in the third strand of the narrative, Satan will resort to insanity as salvation for Fr. Peter.

The conclusion of the second part of the story deals in some detail with the changes that Satan effects in the lives of Nikolaus, Frau Brandt, and Fischer the weaver. Of the three, only Fischer's life is lengthened; the defect in the change is the terrifying implication for Theodor that as a result of his new career Fischer will go to hell. Finally, the vision of human history from its beginning into the future, with no one but a "parcel of unsurping monarchs and nobilities" (p. 234) profiting from life, fortifies the lesson of human misery.

The third strand of the narrative focuses on the trial: Satan's victory for Fr. Peter through the defense by Wilhelm Meidling and the doctrine of laughter that Satan preaches as the only enduring antidote to the absurdities of life. The witch-commission, at first, is afraid to proceed against Fr. Peter and the astrologer—no doubt because of the esteem the village holds for both of them. Instead they hang a poor, friendless woman, while a mob throws stones at her. Satan bursts out laughing, and his laughter is clearly significant. The crowd demands to know why he had laughed and especially why he threw no stone. After answering his three accusers with the announcemnt of their imminent deaths, Satan admits to Theodor that he was actually laughing at him for throwing stones while "his heart revolted at the act" (p. 238). Distrust of neighbor and fear of reprisals had led the mob to be ruled by the malicious few.

When Fr. Peter eventually comes to trial, Satan possesses Wilhelm and, by demonstrating from the date on the coins that they could not belong to the astrologer, wins Fr. Peter's freedom. But the happiness that he had promised Theodor he would gain for Fr. Peter is the happiness of insanity, for he lies to Fr. Peter and tells him that he has been found guilty and been disgraced—and the shock dislodges the old man's reason. When Theodor reproaches Satan for his lie, Satan explains his action: "Are you so unobservant as not to have found out that sanity and happiness are an impossible combination? No sane man can be happy, for to him life is real, and he sees what a fearful thing it is. Only the mad can be happy, and not many of those" (p. 246).

Satan's third discourse follows immediately; it is an explanation of his laughter during the stoning episode as well as a corollary to his observations on insanity and happiness. The human race, he insists, lacks a genuine sense of humor. They see "the comic side of a thousand low-grade and trivial . . . incongruities"—another example of the "continuous and uninterrupted self-deception" that enslaves the race, but they miss thereby "the ten-thousand high-grade comicalities which exist in the world" (p. 247). The only antidote to these radical inconsistencies is to "laugh at them—and by laughing at them destroy them" (*ibid.*). He concludes: "Against the assault of laughter nothing can stand" (pp. 247-48). We understand now the curious rationality behind his salvation of Fr. Peter. Both laughter and insanity negate reality; but since the race lacks the courage to laugh, insanity was the only sure redemption for Fr. Peter.

The excursion to India is the last narrative episode of the story; and although it seems somehow unequal to its climactic position in the narrative, it does nevertheless serve as a summary illustration of Satan's Gospel. The foreigner, a Portuguese colonist, refuses to allow the natives to enjoy the fruit of Satan's tree even for an hour because the tree is on his property. The natives respond with humble obeisance to their master. Only the moral sense can explain the foreigner's perversity, and the misery of the groveling natives is another example of the foolish acceptance of the master-slave relationship "which is the foundation upon which all civilizations have been built" (p. 234). The foreigner will conceal his acceptance of the sentence Satan has imposed upon him—for fear of the natives. Only by preventing their revenge can he secure his ascendancy over them. The "high-grade" incongruity of the foreigner's situation is that he will "fetch a priest to cast out the tree's devil" (p. 251). Of course, the priest's incantations will be ineffectual;

such belief itself is the ultimate incongruity of the race because it is patently groundless.

Before discussing the final chapter in relationship to the narrative as it has unfolded thus far, we must consider the cosmic dimension added to the narrative structure by the threefold excursion into time and space. "It was wonderful," Theodor exclaims at the beginning of Chapter Nine, "the mastery Satan had over time and distance" (p. 235). An overview of Twain's method of universalizing the lessons learned through the process of Fr. Peter's salvation is crucial to a proper understanding of the function of the controversial last chapter.

Each of Satan's three discourses is applied to all of humanity—in space and in time. In the first strand, the journey to the French factory becomes a spatial confirmation of the universal perversity of man's moral sense. The temporal expansion of the discourse is achieved by Satan's symbolic repetition of the creation of the world. The sequence of miracles by which he establishes his angelic powers (which are really more divine than angelic, according to any traditional theological model)—fire, ice, fruit, animals, and finally men—corresponds roughly to the order of creation found in the first chapter of Genesis--—light, firmament, plants, animals, and man. There would seem to be no other reason for this succession of miracles, in precisely this order, than to take us back in time to the very origin of man's problem—his creation as a being endowed with the moral sense.

The setting of the second discourse is China, as far removed from Eseldorf as is spatially conceivable on this planet. We may conjecture that the reason "why Satan chose China for this excursion instead of another place" (p. 210) is that he has thereby encircled the globe with his doctrine of necessary human misery, determined by the very fact of our existence in this world. The temporal excursion during this portion encompasses the whole of human history from Cain through the present and then "two or three centuries" into the future of the race, exhibiting only "a mighty procession" (p. 234) of slaughter and oppression.

The third discourse deals with the capacity of laughter to annul the appalling incongruities of reality. The last spatial excursion is to India and Ceylon; and the episode that occurs is, as we have seen, weakly illustrative of Philip Traum's total vision of the human race. The location, though, suggests the aura of mysticism characteristic of that area of the world—a perfect prelude to the final encounter between Theodor and Satan. The last chapter and its announcement of the dream quality of reality becomes the temporal conclusion to the story. To be fully understood within the structure of the work, it must be seen—in juxtaposition to creation at the beginning of the narrative—as the apocalypse of the end of time. We can see now more clearly, too, the progression from insanity through laughter to dream—since the proclamation that all reality is nothing but a dream is, of course, the theoretical ultimate in this series of views destructive of reality.

Understood as apocalypse, the final chapter both completes the temporal progression of the story and helps us to comprehend the nature of the change that has come over Theodor, because there can be no doubt that there is a qualitative difference between their encounter in the last chapter and their relationship until then. If we trace the development of Theodor's attitude toward Satan through the three stages of the narrative, we find that he moves from a period of profound shock at Satan's indifference to humanity, to a desire to reform Satan's ways, and finally to an attitude of diminished grief and private disapproval of Satan's actions. When Satan's lie has resulted in Fr. Peter's insanity, Theodor reflects: "Privately I did not think much of his processes" (p. 247). And after Satan's punishment of the Portuguese landowner, he admits that it grieved him, "though not sharply, to see [Satan] take such a malicious satisfaction in his plans" (p. 250) for the foreigner. There is no simple linear development in Theodor's acceptance of Satan's shocking vision of humanity.

The level of response that we have traced thus far is primarily concerned with Satan's attitude and the consequent harshness of his actions. Running throughout the story, though, is the far more important motif of the boys' personal attachment to Philip. The enchantment of the person—the lure of his music, the excitement of his presence, and the ecstasy of his wine from heaven—is pronounced from the beginning and only grows in intensity as the story unfolds. "He made us drunk with the joy of being with him, and of looking into the heaven of his eyes, and of feeling the ecstasy that thrilled our veins from the touch of his hand" (p. 171). It is undoubtedly this attachment to the power of Philip's personality that becomes the ground for Theodor's leap of faith in accepting his final revelation.

But Satan himself is a dream and nothing more. How are we to understand this subtler aspect of the final revelation? "I am but a dream—your dream, creature of your imagination. . . . I, your poor servant, have revealed you to yourself and set you free. Dream other dreams, and better!" (p. 252). The dream that has uttered a final and definitive "No!" to reality is a dream that is conditioned by the age of belief—and which denies the reality of God, heaven, hell, the human race, and the universe. What is rejected here by Theodor's imagination is quite simply, but emphatically the Christian explanation of existence. But it is also more than this. It is a rejection of any reality outside of the self. Theodor is nothing more than "a vagrant thought, . . . wandering forlorn among the empty eternities!'' *(ibid.)*. The only better dream, then, that he can presumably dream is laughter.

We are left, finally, with the evident incongruity of an adolescent solipsist. However, even though the first person point of view is used, the story is narrated in the past tense—which indicates the passage of time between the actual occurrence of the events and the time of narration. Despite the fact that an effort is made to maintain the youthful point of view, there are certain passages where the age of the narrator shows through. In the opening paragraph, the narrator indicates that the Austria of the story is a remembrance, but that he remembers it well even though he was "only a boy" (p. 161). In recalling his last days with Nick, he notes: "It was an awful eleven days; and yet, with a lifetime stretching back between today and then, they are still a grateful memory to me, and beautiful" (p. 222). In Chapter Ten, while commenting on the fact that Satan seemed to know of no other way to do a person a favor except "by killing him or making a lunatic out of him," he adds :"Privately, I did not think much of his processes—*at that time*" (p. 247, my emphasis). And during Satan's final revelation, there is the patently adult exclamation: "By God! I had had that very thought a thousand times in my musings" (p. 252). Rather than consider these as lapses from the established viewpoint, as some critics have done, it seems more reasonable to explain them as intended emphasis of the passage of time. It certainly makes it easier for us to understand and accept the final vision of reality if we realize that it is an old man who is reflecting the bitterness of age, or at least a process of many years.

If Mark Twain has treated us to a harshly solipsistic view of reality, he has not done so without a sense of humor. Moreover, he has sweetened his anti-Gospel with the nostalgia of youth and given the vision artistic distance by setting the story in the remote past of our belief. And then he has, of course, left us with laughter.

Annotated Bibliography

MARK TWAIN'S PRINCIPAL WORKS

The Celebrated Jumping Frog of Calaveras County, and Other Sketches, 1867.
The Innocents Abroad, 1869.
Roughing It, 1872.
The Gilded Age (with Charles Dudley Warner), 1873.
Mark Twain's Sketches, New and Old, 1875.
The Adventures of Tom Sawyer, 1876.
A True Story and the Recent Carnival of Crime, 1877
Punch, Brothers, Punch!, 1878.
A Tramp Abroad, 1880.
The Prince and the Pauper, 1882.
The Stolen White Elephant, 1882.
Life on the Mississippi, 1883.
Adventures of Huckleberry Finn, 1885.
A Connecticut Yankee in King Arthur's Court, 1889.
The American Claimant, 1892.
Merry Tales, 1892.
The £ 1,000,000 Bank Note and Other New Stories, 1893.
Tom Sawyer Abroad, 1894.
The Tragedy of Pudd'nhead Wilson and the Comedy of Those Extraordinary Twins, 1894.
Personal Recollections of Joan of Arc, 1896.
Tom Sawyer Abroad, Tom Sawyer, Detective, and Other Stories, 1896.
Following the Equator, 1897.
How to Tell a Story and Other Essays, 1897.
The Man that Corrupted Hadleyburg and Other Stories and Essays, 1900.
A Double Barrelled Detective Story, 1902.
My Début as a Literary Person, 1903.
A Dog's Tale, 1904.
Extracts from Adam's Diary, 1904.

King Leopold's Soliloquy, 1905.
The $30,000 Bequest and Other Stories, 1906.
Eve's Diary, 1906.
Christian Science, 1907.
A Horse's Tale, 1907.
Is Shakespeare Dead?, 1909.
Extract from Captain Stormfield's Visit to Heaven, 1909.
The Mysterious Stranger, 1916.
What is Man? and Other Essays, 1917.
The Curious Republic of Gondour, 1919.
Europe and Elsewhere, 1923.

COLLECTED WORKS

So many editions of the collected works have been published that there would be little point in listing all of them here. The edition most favored by specialists is the "definitive edition": *The Writings of Mark Twain,* ed. Albert Bigelow Paine, 37 vols. (New York: Gabriel Wells, 1922–25). The "Stormfield edition" was printed from the same plates in 1929.

In the process of publication is the "Iowa-California edition" of *The Works of Mark Twain* from the University of California Press. When completed, this twenty-five volume, uniform edition will include all of Mark Twain's published books along with related material from his writings.

The University of California Press is also publishing in a uniform edition fifteen volumes of the Mark Twain Papers. These volumes will include incomplete literary manuscripts, notebooks, correspondence, and other documents, most of them previously unpublished. The volumes now available are listed below under the appropriate headings, either "Letters" or "Miscellaneous Writings."

Miscellaneous Writings of Mark Twain

Mark Twain's Speeches. New York: Harper and Bros., 1910.
Mark Twain's Autobiography. Edited by Albert Bigelow Paine. 2 vols. New York: Harper and Bros., 1924.
Mark Twain's Notebook. Edited by Albert Bigelow Paine. New York: Harper and Bros., 1935.
Letters from the Sandwich Islands, written for The Sacramento Union by Mark Twain. Edited by G. Ezra Dane. Stanford, Calif.: Stanford University Press, 1938.

Letters from Honolulu, written for the Sacramento Union by Mark Twain. Honolulu: Nickerson, 1939.

Mark Twain's Travels with Mr. Brown: Sketches for the San Francisco Alta California, 1866–67. Edited by Franklin Walker and G. Ezra Dane. New York: Knopf, 1940.

Mark Twain in Eruption. Edited by Bernard De Voto. New York: Harper and Bros., 1940.

Mark Twain's Letters in the Muscatine Journal. Edited by Edgar M. Branch. Chicago: Mark Twain Association of America, 1942.

The Letters of Quintus Curtius Snodgrass. Edited by Ernest E. Leisy. Dallas: Southern Methodist University Press, 1946.

Mark Twain of the Enterprise: Newspaper Articles and Other Documents, 1862–1864. Edited by Henry Nash Smith and Frederick Anderson. Berkeley: University of California Press, 1957.

Traveling with the Innocents Abroad: Mark Twain's Original Reports from Europe and the Holy Land. Edited by Daniel Morley McKeithan. Norman: University of Oklahoma Press, 1958.

The Autobiography of Mark Twain. Edited by Charles Neider. New York: Harper and Bros., 1959.

Contributions to the Galaxy. Edited by Bruce McElderry. Gainesville, Fla.: Scholars' Facsimiles and Reprints, 1961.

Letters from the Earth. Edited by Bernard De Voto. New York: Harper and Bros., 1962.

Mark Twain's San Francisco. Edited by Bernard Taper. New York: McGraw-Hill, 1963.

Mark Twain's Letters from Hawaii. Edited by A. Grove Day. New York: Appleton-Century, 1966.

Mark Twain's Satires and Burlesques. Edited by Franklin R. Rogers. Berkeley: University of California Press, 1967.

Mark Twain's "Which Was the Dream?" and Other Symbolic Writings of the Later Years. Edited by John S. Tuckey. Berkeley: University of California Press, 1967.

Mark Twain's Mysterious Stranger *Manuscripts.* Edited by William M. Gibson. Berkeley: University of California Press, 1969.

Mark Twain's Hannibal: Huck and Tom. Edited by Walter Blair. Berkeley: University of California Press, 1970.

Mark Twain's Fables of Man. Edited by John S. Tuckey. Berkeley: University of California Press, 1972.

Mark Twain's Notebooks and Journals, vol. I (1855–73). Edited by Frederick Anderson, Michael B. Frank, and Kenneth M. Sanderson. Vol. II (1877–83), edited by Frederick Anderson, Lin Salamo, and Bernard L. Stein. Berkeley: University of California Press, 1974.

Letters

Mark Twain's Letters. Edited by Albert Bigelow Paine. 2 vols. New York: Harper and Bros., 1917.

Mark Twain's Letters to Will Bowen. Edited by Theodore Hornberger. Austin: University of Texas Press, 1941.

Mark Twain, Business Man. Edited by Samuel C. Webster. Boston: Little, Brown, 1946.

The Love Letters of Mark Twain. Edited by Dixon Wector. New York: Harper and Bros., 1949.

Mark Twain to Mrs. Fairbanks. Edited by Dixon Wector. San Marino, Calif.: Huntington Library, 1949.

Mark Twain-Howells Letters: The Correspondence of Samuel L. Clemens and William Dean Howells. Edited by Henry Nash Smith, William M. Gibson and Frederick Anderson. Boston: Harvard University Press, 1960. (A one-volume edition, *Selected Mark Twain-Howells Letters,* 1967).

Mark Twain's Letters to Mary. Edited by Lewis Leary. New York: Columbia University Press, 1961.

Mark Twain's Letters to his Publishers, 1867–1894. Edited by Hamlin Hill. Berkeley: University of California Press, 1967.

Mark Twain's Correspondence with Henry Huttleston Rogers: 1893–1909. Edited by Lewis Leary. Berkeley: University of California Press, 1970.

BIBLIOGRAPHIES

Mark Twain's Works

Blanck, Jacob. *Bibliography of American Literature,* vol. II. New Haven, Conn.: Yale University Press; London: Oxford University Press, 1957.

Johnson, Merle. *A Bibliography of the Works of Mark Twain, Samuel Langhorne Clemens*. Rev. ed. New York: Harper and Bros., 1935.

Writings about Mark Twain

Asselineau, Roger. *The Literary Reputation of Mark Twain from 1910 to 1950: A Critical Essay and a Bibliography*. Paris: Libraire Marcel Didier, 1954; New York: Gregory Lounz, 1956.

Beebe, Maurice, and John Feaster. "Criticism of Mark Twain: A Selected Checklist," *Modern Fiction Studies,* XIV (Spring, 1968), 93–139.

Leary, Lewis. *Articles on American Literature,* 1900–1950. Durham, N.C.: Duke University Press, 1954.

———, with Carolyn Bartholet, and Catharine Roth. *Articles on American Literature,* 1950–1967. Durham, N.C.: Duke University Press, 1970.

Spiller, Robert *et al.,* eds. | *Literary History of the United States, 4th ed.* New York: Macmillan, 1974. See *Bibliography.*

Wagenknecht, Edward. "Bibliography" and "A Commentary on Mark Twain Criticism and Scholarship since 1960," *Mark Twain: The Man and His Work.* Norman: University of Oklahoma Press, 1967.

Woodress, James, ed. *Eight American Authors: A Review of Research and Criticism.* Rev. ed. New York: W.W. Norton, 1971. Contains a Mark Twain section by Harry Hayden Clark, pp. 273–320.

ANNUALS

American Literary Scholarship: An Annual. Durham, N.C.: Duke University Press. This review of scholarship and criticism always contains a section on Mark Twain.

MLA Abstracts. New York: Modern Language Association. Contains short abstracts of important journal articles. Recommended for use with the concurrent *MLA International Bibliography.*

MLA International Bibliography. New York: Modern Language Association. A comprehensive listing of books and articles published each year.

In the following secondary works, the division into the general categories of biography and criticism has sometimes been made according to emphasis since many of the books contain both biographical and critical material.

A selection from the extensive material on Mark Twain printed in journals has not been included. Readers interested in examining this literature may consult the Bibliographies section under the heading "Writings about Mark Twain": all entries there list articles.

Two journals specialize in publishing articles and information about Mark Twain: *The Twainian,* published by the Mark Twain Research Foundation, and *The Mark Twain Journal,* published by the Mark Twain Memorial Association.

BIOGRAPHY

Allen, Jerry. *The Adventures of Mark Twain*. Boston: Little, Brown, 1954.

Andrews, Kenneth R. *Nook Farm: Mark Twain's Hartford Circle*. Cambridge, Mass: Harvard University Press, 1950. An account of Mark Twain's life, work, and friends during the twenty years (1871–91) he lived in the intellectual community of Nook Farm, Hartford, Conn.

Benson, Ivan. *Mark Twain's Western Years*. Stanford, Calif.: Stanford University Press, 1938. The five and a half years (1861–66) spent in Nevada and California.

Brashear, Minnie M. *Mark Twain: Son of Missouri*. Chapel Hill: University of North Carolina Press, 1934. This book sets out to show that the early years in Hannibal provided a higher level of cultural influences than generally assumed.

Brooks, Van Wyck. *The Ordeal of Mark Twain*. New York: E. P. Dutton, 1920. Rev. ed., 1933. An influential and controversial study, now largely discounted, proposing that the moralistic pressure of family, friends, and American culture thwarted Mark Twain's genius.

Canby, Henry Seidel. *Turn West, Turn East: Mark Twain and Henry James*. Boston: Houghton Mifflin, 1951. A biographical comparison of the two authors.

Cardwell, Guy A. *Twins of Genius*. East Lansing: Michigan State University Press, 1953. Examines the relationship with G. W. Cable and reprints eighteen letters by Mark Twain and twenty by Cable.

Clemens, Clara. *My Father: Mark Twain*. New York: Harper and Bros., 1931.

De Voto, Bernard. *Mark Twain's America*. Boston: Little, Brown, 1932. In maintaining that Mark Twain's genius was well served by his American background, this book gained notoriety for its heavy attack on Van Wyck Brooks' methods and conclusions in the book listed previously.

Duckett, Margaret. *Mark Twain and Bret Harte*. Norman: University of Oklahoma Press, 1964.

Fatout, Paul. *Mark Twain in Virginia City*. Bloomington: Indiana University Press, 1964.

———. *Mark Twain on the Lecture Circuit*. Bloomington: Indiana University Press, 1960.

Ferguson, DeLancey. *Mark Twain: Man and Legend*. Indianapolis: Bobbs-Merrill, 1943. An excellent biography covering the full life.

Frear, Walter Francis. *Mark Twain and Hawaii*. Privately printed, Lakeside Press, 1947, Includes much material by Mark Twain.

Ganzel, Dewey. *Mark Twain Abroad: The Cruise of the Quaker City*. Chicago: University of Chicago Press, 1968. On the 1867 excursion to Europe and the Holy Land.

Henderson, Archibald. *Mark Twain*. New York: Frederick A. Stokes, 1910. An early general study.

Hill, Hamlin. *Mark Twain and Elisha Bliss*. Columbia: University of Missouri Press, 1964. An account of Mark Twain's relationship with the publisher and the American Publishing Co.

———. *Mark Twain: God's Fool*. New York: Harper and Row, 1973. A full account of the final ten years of the author's life.

Howells, William Dean. *My Mark Twain: Reminiscences and Criticisms*. Edited by Marilyn A. Baldwin. Baton Rouge: Louisiana State University Press, 1967. A new edition of the affectionate memorial by his loyal friend, including the reviews reprinted in the original volume. First published in 1910.

Kaplan, Justin. *Mr. Clemens and Mark Twain*. New York: Simon and Schuster, 1966. A detailed account of his life, beginning in 1866 at age thirty.

Lawton, Mary. *A Lifetime with Mark Twain, The Memories of Katy Leary, For Thirty Years His Faithful and Devoted Servant*. New York: Harcourt Brace, 1925.

Meltzer, Milton. *Mark Twain Himself: A Pictorial Biography*. New York: Thomas Y. Crowell, 1960. A rich pictorial collection of Mark Twain and his times, with accompanying text.

Paine, Albert Bigelow. *Mark Twain: A Biography*. 3 vols. New York: Harper and Bros., 1912. The authorized biography, a valuable source that needs supplementing from the corrections and additions of later biographers.

Salsbury, Edith Colgate, ed. *Family Dialogue: Susy and Mark Twain*. New York: Harper and Row, 1965. Writings arranged in dialogue form to portray the Clemens family.

Scott, Arthur L. *Mark Twain at Large*. Chicago: Henry Regnery, 1969. A book about Mark Twain's travels and his opinions on the foreign scene.

Turner, Arlin. *Mark Twain and G. W. Cable: The Record of a Literary Friendship*. East Lansing: Michigan State University Press, 1960. Mostly Cable's letters, supplemented with some letters by Mark Twain.

Wagenknecht, Edward. *Mark Twain: The Man and his Work*. 3rd ed. Norman: University of Oklahoma Press, 1967. Originally published in 1935, this full study remains one of the most informative accounts. Includes a useful bibliography and critical survey of scholarship and criticism.

Wector, Dixon. *Sam Clemens of Hannibal.* Boston: Houghton Mifflin, 1952. A biography of the early years.

CRITICISM

Anderson, Frederick, ed. with Kenneth M. Sanderson. *Mark Twain: The Critical Heritage.* New York: Barnes & Noble, 1971. Reviews of Mark Twain's work, from 1869 to 1913.

Baetzhold, H. G. *Mark Twain and John Bull: The British Connection.* Bloomington: Indiana University Press, 1970. An account of Mark Twain's varied relationship with England, Englishmen, and English literature.

Baldanza, Frank. *Mark Twain: An Introduction and Interpretation.* New York: Barnes & Noble, 1961. A brief introduction to the man and his work.

Bellamy, Gladys Carmen. *Mark Twain as a Literary Artist.* Norman: University of Oklahoma Press, 1950. The first full length study of Mark Twain as a conscious artist.

Blair, Walter. *Mark Twain & Huck Finn.* Berkeley: University of California Press, 1960. A study of all the forces that went into the making of *Huckleberry Finn.*

Blues, Thomas. *Mark Twain and the Community.* Lexington: University of Kentucky Press, 1970. Sums up Twain's attitudes about the relationship of the individual with his society.

Branch, Edgar Marquess. *The Literary Apprenticeship of Mark Twain: With Selections from his Apprentice Writing.* Urbana: University of Illinois Press, 1950. An account of his early career.

Budd, Louis J. *Mark Twain, Social Philosopher.* Bloomington: Indiana University Press, 1962. Assesses the social, economic, and political ideas, concluding that Mark Twain was more often conservative than is generally believed.

Cardwell, Guy A., ed. *Discussions of Mark Twain.* Boston: D.C. Heath, 1963. A collection of critical material.

Covici, Pascal, Jr. *Mark Twain's Humor.* Dallas: Southern Methodist University Press, 1962. A study of humor as a conscious literary device.

Cox, James M. *Mark Twain: The Fate of Humor.* Princeton, N.J.: Princeton University Press, 1966. Contends that Mark Twain's work was successful when he followed his comic genius and unsuccessful when he tried to be serious.

De Voto, Bernard. *Mark Twain at Work*. Cambridge, Mass.: Harvard University Press, 1942. This book contains three essays about Mark Twain, as well as previously unpublished manuscript material.

Ensar, Allison. *Mark Twain and the Bible*. Lexington: University Press of Kentucky, 1970.

Foner, Philip S. *Mark Twain, Social Critic*. New York: International Publishers, 1958.

French, Bryant Morley. *Mark Twain and the Gilded Age: The Book that Named an Era*. Dallas: Southern Methodist University Press, 1965.

Geismar, Maxwell. *Mark Twain: An American Prophet*. Boston: Houghton Mifflin, 1970. An eccentric general study.

Grant, Douglas. *Mark Twain*. Edinburgh: Oliver and Boyd; New York: Grove Press, 1962. A brief introduction to the man and his work.

Hemminghaus, Edgar T. *Mark Twain in Germany*. New York: Columbia University Press, 1939. On Mark Twain's influence after 1874.

Kaplan, Justin, ed. *Mark Twain: A Profile*. New York: Hill and Wang, 1967. A collection of critical essays.

Krause, Sydney J. *Mark Twain as Critic*. Baltimore: Johns Hopkins Press, 1967. A study of Mark Twain's literary criticism.

Krumpelmann, John T. *Mark Twain and the German Language*. Baton Rouge: Louisiana State University Press, 1953.

Leary, Lewis. *Mark Twain*. Minneapolis: University of Minnesota Press, 1960. No. 5 in the "Pamphlets on American Writers" series.

———, ed. *A Casebook on Mark Twain's Wound*. New York: Thomas Y. Crowell, 1962. A collection of essays selected to throw light on the Brooks-DeVoto controversy.

Long, E. Hudson. *Mark Twain Handbook*. New York: Hendricks House, 1957. A summary of his life, backgrounds, career, art, ideas, and reputation.

Lorch, Fred W. *The Trouble Begins at Eight: Mark Twain's Lecture Tours*. Ames: Iowa State University Press, 1965. With a focus on Twain's manners and style as a lecturer.

Lynn, Kenneth S. *Mark Twain and Southwestern Humor*. Boston: Little, Brown, 1960. Places Twain in a humorous tradition and interprets major works.

Neider, Charles. *Mark Twain*. New York: Horizon Press, 1967. Most of the chapters in this book were originally published as introductions to collections of Mark Twain's writings.

Regan, Robert. *Unpromising Heroes: Mark Twain and His Characters*. Berkeley: University of California Press, 1966. Presents the thesis that a number of Twain's characters follow the pattern of the traditional figure in folklore who win success against all expectations.

Rogers, Franklin R. *Mark Twain's Burlesque Patterns, as seen in the Novels and Narratives,* 1855–1885. Dallas: Southern Methodist University Press, 1960.

Rowlette, Robert. *Mark Twain's "Pudd'nhead Wilson."* Bowling Green, Ohio: Bowling Green University Popular Press, 1971.

Salomon, Roger B. *Twain and the Image of History.* New Haven, Conn.: Yale University Press, 1961. On Mark Twain's historical ideas and writings.

Scott, Arthur L., ed. *Mark Twain: Selected Criticism.* Rev. ed. Dallas: Southern Methodist University Press, 1967. Selections from 1867 to 1963.

——. *On the Poetry of Mark Twain: With Selections from his Verse.* Urbana: University of Illinois Press, 1966. Examines a minor but intriguing aspect of Twain's literary work and prints sixty-five of the 120 poems known to have been written.

Simpson, Claude A. *Twentieth Century Interpretations of the Adventures of Huckleberry Finn.* Englewood Cliffs, N.J.: Prentice-Hall, 1968. A collection of critical essays.

Smith, Henry Nash, ed. *Mark Twain.* Englewood Cliffs, N.J.: Prentice-Hall, 1963. A collection of critical essays.

——. *Mark Twain: The Development of a Writer.* Cambridge, Mass.: Harvard University Press, 1962. A study of style, structure, and meaning traced through nine of the major works.

——. *Mark Twain's Fable of Progress: Political and Economic Ideas in "A Connecticut Yankee."* New Brunswick, N.J.: Rutgers University Press, 1964.

Spengemann, William C. *Mark Twain and the Backwoods Angel: The Matter of Innocence in the Works of Samuel L. Clemens.* Kent, Ohio: Kent State University Press, 1966. Examines Twain's concern with the problem of American innocence.

Stone, Albert E. *The Innocent Eye: Childhood in Mark Twain's Imagination.* New Haven, Conn.: Yale University Press, 1961.

Tuckey, John S. *Mark Twain and Little Satan: The Writings of "The Mysterious Stranger."* West Lafayette, Ind.: Purdue University Studies, 1963. This analysis of *The Mysterious Stranger* carries out a rigorous textual criticism and reconstructs the composition of the novel.

Wiggins, Robert A. *Mark Twain: Jackleg Novelist.* Seattle: University of Washington Press, 1964. Pursues the notion that Mark Twain's novels were improvised rather than the product of a deliberate craft. "Jackleg" was a nineteenth-century term meaning an impostor or incompetent workman.